Better Than Take-Out

(& Faster, Too)

Quick and easy cooking for busy families

Pamela Marx
Illustrated by Matthew D. Wittmer

D1262010

PERSPECTIVE
PUBLISHING

LOS ANGELES

Published by Perspective Publishing, Inc.
2528 Sleepy Hollow Dr. #A, Glendale, CA 91206
800-330-5851; 818-502-1270; fax: 818-502-1272;
books@familyhelp.com
www.familyhelp.com

Additional copies of this book may be ordered by calling toll free
1-800-330-5851, or by sending $18.95 ($14.95 + $4 shipping) to the above
address. CA residents add 8% ($1.20) sales tax. Discounts available for
quantity orders. Bookstores, please call LPC Group at 1-800-626-4330.

Library of Congress Cataloging-in-Publication Data

Marx, Pamela
    Better than take-out (& faster, too) : quick and easy cooking for busy families
    / Pamela Marx : Illustrated by Matthew D. Wittmer—1st ed.
        p. cm.
    Includes index.
    ISBN 1-930085-02-8
        1. Cookery, American. 2.Quick and easy cookery. I. Title

TX715 .M3693 2001
641.5'55—dc21

                                            2001036218

Illustrations by Matthew D. Wittmer
Printed in the United States
First Edition

To Mark

and to Lisa, Martha, and Rhonda

Grateful acknowledgments for recipe ideas, testing and support go to Lisa Skylar, Fred Wyatt, Mark Goldstein, Megan Goldstein, Holly Goldstein, Norma Marx, Bill Marx, Eileen Hatrick, Martha Gustafson, Linda Pillsbury, Steve Hopkinson, Rhonda Heth, Fumiko Makishima, Julianna Kosakowski, Mojca Rasmussen, Bev Lipka, Gail Eaton, Debbie Mansfield, Sara Gordon, Margaret Villarreal, Lena Bennett, Karen Van Bremen, Debbie Vodhanel, Mary Jean Goldstein, Phineas Goldstein, and to all the readers who shared their time to review and try recipes.

Table of Contents

It IS Better Than Take-Out

We're all too busy to cook, but we like a good meal or snack. Too often, between soccer practice and trumpet lessons and homework, we just stop by the local drive-thru. At the end of the week when we find that we've stopped three times, we're sure that just can't be. Have we become a statistic?

This cookbook is designed to give busy people like us quick, yet tasty, recipe ideas to serve both for daily meals and special events. Most of the recipes really are faster than picking up take-out when you consider drive and wait time. There are lots of main dishes that can be on the table in 10 or 15 minutes and they are certainly healthier than take-out. If you have a handful of new ideas for dinner, you might find it less daunting to throw something together at home rather than breaking a ten (or a twenty) at the drive-thru.

Many of these recipes came from friends, family members, and acquaintances who shared recipes for their quickest dinner meals. Others came from oft-tested office potluck favorites. Still others are old-and-easy recipes we knew but have forgotten. Of course, not every meal fits every family, but if one doesn't work for the dining tastes in your home, hopefully the next one will. There is something for everyone since each friend or relative who gave ideas for this book has his or her own picky eaters.

As busy as we get, it's nice to be able to put a little something new on the table or to have a quick interesting dish at hand to serve for special events.

Quick Tips

The purpose of this cookbook is to help busy people find quick and easy ways to put satisfying, tasty meals and snacks on the table without spending a lot of time in the kitchen. Therefore, it makes sense to think of as many ways as possible to cut down on time spent in the kitchen. This section provides information on the timesaving tips used to prepare the recipes in this book in the times indicated as well as general tips for decreasing time spent on food preparation.

Timesavers

When gauging how much time is needed to prepare a dish, it is important to know which short cuts I relied upon and built into the preparation times listed for the recipes. These include the following:

* Except in the case of cheeses that don't come pre-shredded or grated such as Gruyère and Gorgonzola, buy shredded cheese in bags.

* When shredded cabbage is called for, use a bag of coleslaw.

* Consider quick alternatives to chopping and mincing onion and garlic. For onion, use a bag of fresh chopped onion available in the produce section of the market or frozen chopped onion available in the frozen foods section. A jar of crushed garlic is a very handy alternative to fresh garlic. For a quick way to peel and mince fresh garlic, cut off the ends of the clove, smash it with the side of a knife or cleaver to break the skin, peel the skin off and mince it by making checkerboard cuts into the clove through which you slice sideways. If this doesn't work for you, use that handy jar of crushed garlic.

* I use almost no special equipment such as food processors or blenders when making food for any occasion. I don't want to clean the equipment because I don't like doing dishes. The one piece of equipment sometimes referred to in the recipes is a potato masher which I prefer to something

fancier. Where a blender or food processor would work much better than a potato masher, I have referenced this in the tips that follow many of the recipes.

* When doing a vegetable sauté, I almost never cut my vegetables first on a cutting board and then put them into the pan. I put the oil on and chop the onion right into the pan. (The same goes for garlic and I haven't lost any fingers yet, although this is not a method for children to use.) I add softer vegetables when the onions are translucent by chopping these directly into the pan as well. If you are not comfortable with this, your cooking time may be a few minutes longer than that indicated, but it shouldn't vary by much.

Rice

Obviously, one of the fastest ways to get something that passes for rice on the table is to use a minute-style rice, but for those who prefer the taste and texture of less refined types of rice, there are some other methods to try. First, you might consider investing in an electric rice cooker. Rice cooks quickly with no attention required and it keeps warm until you are ready to serve it. For help cooking specific kinds of rice, consider the following:

Basmati Rice: This is an excellent rice, but can be a long and tricky job when cooking it stove-top. Instead, do it in the microwave. While you are fixing your ten-minute meal stove-top, your basmati is cooking in the same time on the other side of the Atlantic in the microwave. For 1 cup basmati, add 2 cups water. Put it in a microwave safe bowl and cover. I usually just lay a plate on top of the plastic mixing bowl. Heat it on high for about 9 minutes. Depending upon the size and material of your container, it should be more or less done at this point. If it needs a little more time, continue cooking for a minute or two.

Wild Rice—I have yet to find a real fast way to cook up wild rice. Whether in the microwave or stove-top, it seems to take an awful long time. You can use 3 cups water to 1 cup wild rice and cook it using the same method as described for basmati rice above except that the cooking time is between 20 and 25 minutes. Once you have invested this much time in the cooking, maximize the effort by freezing the results in 1/2 to 1 cup increments in freezer bags. Then you can use wild rice whenever you want by defrosting it in the microwave. Add 1/2 to 1 cup wild rice to 2 or 3 cups cooked white rice for a tasty, nutritious side dish. Seasoned with garlic powder, green onions, and a bit of butter, it's a winner.

4~Quick Tips

Pasta

Pasta preparation time depends upon the type of pasta you choose to use. Here are some timesaver ideas for pasta.

Capellini, Angel Hair and Fideos: If you want to prepare a quick pasta for a main dish or a side dish, one of these thin string pastas is a great choice. They cook up in about three minutes, once the water is boiling. These are not good pastas for freezing and reusing later.

Fusilli, Corkscrew, Elbow, Bow Tie, Penne: These pastas take longer to cook—between 7 and 10 minutes, depending upon the one you choose. They are, however, sometimes the best choice for the dish you want to make. If you plan to use them for your quick pasta dish, make sure you start the water as soon you begin preparing the other ingredients. Then, the pasta will be ready about the same time you have finished with chopping and cooking the vegetables or making your sauce—about 15 minutes, max.

Another way to make these pastas user-friendly is to cook them ahead of time and freeze them in gallon size plastic bags for reheating later. To do this, drain the pasta well and rinse with cold water so that it is room temperature. Freeze it in a plastic pouch—about 2 cups to a pouch. To heat for use, put the bag in the microwave cracked open for air to escape and heat on high for 2 1/2 minutes. Move it around a bit and heat on high again for 2 1/2 minutes. It should be ready to serve. Rinse with hot water and use in your dish. This method allows you to have thick pasta ready to use in five minutes. Some cooks may like this method. Others will prefer cooking pasta fresh when they plan to serve it.

Potatoes

If you want to make potatoes for potato salad or other chopped potato dishes, do not boil the whole potato and then rinse, cool and chop. This method is very time consuming. To be as efficient as possible, chop your potatoes (with the skin on—it never hurt anyone) and drop them into the boiling water already at the size you plan to use. When they are done, rinse them in cold water. They both cook and cool more quickly this way. Be careful not to cook to mush unless you want to use them to make mashed potatoes, in which case you may want to peel them first.

Other Useful Tips

As you look through the recipes, you may have some questions about lowfat or other healthy substitutes you can use for listed ingredients. Consider these ideas:

*   Feel free to use lowfat sour cream and imitation mayonnaise when sour cream and mayonnaise are called for in a recipe.

*   When milk is an ingredient, you can use nonfat milk unless otherwise noted. I have not had lowfat or even 1 percent milk in the house for years and rely on nonfat milk as my cooking ingredient with rare exceptions.

*   While a recipe may call for a tablespoon of oil in the pan when browning onions and the like, I actually dispense with the oil when I cook at home. I put the vegetables in a hot pan and keep them moving until they are done. Then I add my remaining ingredients. You can use this dry pan method if you like or use a little oil or butter in the pan when you brown vegetables. Also, I never add any oil to the pan when I brown meat of any kind. If the pan is too dry, I add a bit of water to keep it from scorching.

Using this Book

Each recipe is set up to provide the basics: ingredient listing, directions, and preparation time. As to the number of diners each recipe serves, this is often not clearly stated. Generally, if it is not identified, a recipe will serve a family of 4. Soups generally feed 4 to 6, if not otherwise noted.

The recipe ingredient quantities are identified as follows:

Cup	c
Tablespoon	T
Teaspoon	t
Pound	lb
Ounce	oz
Package	pkg

Cook as You Are

You can get a quick dinner out of practically anything—a little of this, a little of that and supper's ready. Using the ideas here and whatever is in your cupboard, your family will think you have been planning dinner all day.

Main Dish Mania

Beans, Beans, Beans

If the people in your family will eat beans, there are many fast versions of dinner to rush onto the table.

Red Beans and Rice

Ingredients

1 onion, chopped

1 celery stalk, chopped

Garlic powder

Oil

Cooked sausage

Kidney beans

Rice

Parsley

Directions

Use 1 to 2 cups leftover rice or minute-style rice. In a large skillet, sauté onion, celery, and minced garlic (or use garlic powder) in oil. When vegetables are soft, add a can of drained kidney beans and medallions of cooked sausage of your choice and stir. Mash beans slightly. Add cooked rice and sprinkle with parsley, salt and hot sauce to taste. Stir until warm and serve.

Hoppin' John

Ingredients

1 c cooked rice (leftovers, minute-style, etc.)

1 onion, chopped

1/2 c chopped meat (e.g., ham, bacon, bacon bits, lunch meat)

Can of black-eyed peas

Directions

Cook up a half cup or so of quick rice in the microwave or stove top. You'll want at least a cup of cooked rice. In a separate pan, sauté onion in oil until soft. Add cubed ham (small pieces of lunch meat work fine), cooked bacon, bacon bits (if you like them), or chopped proscuitto and a can of drained black-eyed peas. Sprinkle generously with garlic powder, parsley flakes, salt and pepper. Add rice. Stir until well mixed and heated through. Spice it up with a splash of hot pepper sauce.

Beef and Beans

Ingredients

1 onion, chopped

Garlic powder

Ground beef or pork

Black beans

Cumin

Chili powder

Salt

White rice

Directions

Brown onion, 1 teaspoon garlic powder and about a pound of ground meat over medium high heat. Add 1 can drained black beans and season with cumin, chili powder, salt and pepper. If you prefer, season meat and beans with a package of taco or chili seasoning mix. Stir well to heat through and serve with white rice. Or, roll bean and meat mixture into a large flour tortilla, top with shredded lettuce, chopped tomato, cheese and salsa, and eat as a burrito on the run.

Country-Style Three Bean Blend

Ingredients

1 can butter beans

1 can red beans

1 can kidney beans

1 onion

Ham or Canadian bacon

Catsup

Mustard

Brown sugar

Directions

Open and drain the beans. Reserve some red bean or butter bean liquid. Brown chopped onion and small pieces of ham or Canadian bacon in oil. Add some of the bean liquid with a large squirt of catsup, small squirt of mustard and some brown sugar. (You can adjust the brown sugar and catsup to taste. Start with less brown sugar and add more if you like your beans sweeter.) Stir over medium heat to melt sugar. Add all the beans, stir to blend, and heat through. Serve with minute-style rice and coleslaw or a green salad.

Black Beans and Couscous

Ingredients

Couscous, about 2 cups cooked

1 onion

Garlic (2 minced cloves or 1 t powder)

1 can black beans

1/3 c raisins, dried fruit bits or drained crushed pineapple

Oil

Directions

Follow box directions to cook up couscous. While the couscous is steaming, sauté onion and minced garlic in a little oil. Add a can of drained black beans and a third to a half cup raisins, dried fruit bits or drained crushed pineapple. Heat these ingredients through. Fluff couscous with a fork. Serve bean mixture over couscous with sliced fruit or a green salad on the side.

In the Pot

Two quick hearty soup ideas that are sure to please have a southwestern flavor.

In-a-Jiffy Chili

Ingredients

1/2-1 lb ground beef or turkey

1 chopped onion

Garlic powder, salt and pepper

1 27-oz can drained kidney beans

1 28-oz can pureed tomatoes or tomato sauce

Chili seasoning (or blend of chili powder, cumin, parsley, and oregano)

Directions

Brown meat with chopped onion, garlic powder, salt, and pepper. When the meat is cooked, add drained kidney beans and stewed tomatoes. Season with a packet of chili seasoning and stir to warm through. If you don't have chili seasoning, season with chili powder, cumin, parsley and a little oregano. Dinner is on in 10 minutes with bread and salad on the side. Serve chili with fresh chopped onions and grated cheddar cheese, if desired. For fire-eaters, spice it up with a dash of hot sauce.

Corn Chowder

Ingredients

1 onion

1/2 red bell pepper (optional)

4 T butter (1/2 stick)

1 17-oz can kernel corn

2 17-oz cans creamed corn

1-2 c milk

Salt and pepper

Directions

Brown chopped onion and bell pepper in butter (or margarine). When the vegetables are soft, add the kernel corn (drained), the creamed corn, and a cup or two of milk. Salt and pepper to taste and dinner is ready. If your family does not like bell pepper, you can omit it, but it makes a nice garnish and with a sprig of cilantro you can serve this soup for a festive occasion.

Stretching Rice

If you eat Chinese out and have leftover rice, always bring it home because it's worth a second meal.

Sort-of Fried Rice

Ingredients

4 c cooked white rice

1 onion, chopped

2 cloves garlic (minced) or 1 t garlic powder

1 t fresh ginger root (minced) or 1/2 t ginger powder

Chopped or small vegetables

Oil

Nuts

Soy sauce

Directions

To begin, brown onion and garlic in a tablespoon or two of vegetable oil. Add minced fresh ginger root, if you have it—ground ginger powder, if you don't. Add any chopped vegetables you have such as small pieces of broccoli, frozen corn or succotash, frozen peas and carrots, fresh chopped zucchini and the like. Stir fry vegetables in medium hot oil quickly until softened. Lower heat and add rice; break rice up into vegetables. Add a tablespoon or two of water if rice is dry. Sprinkle with soy sauce and toss in sliced almonds, peanuts or cashews, drained pineapple tidbits (also called snack wedges) and/or cooked, cubed leftover chicken, ham or shrimp. Stir all ingredients to warm through. Splash with sesame oil just before serving if you have it.

* If you want to keep rice vegetarian, use only vegetables or toss in an egg and scramble it quickly in a corner of the pan. Then mix it into the rest of the fried rice. Diners can season the fried rice with an extra splash of soy sauce, if they choose. Serve with fresh fruit and a green salad.

Main Dish Mess

Ingredients

Cooked rice or noodles

1 onion, chopped

Cooked, chopped meat

Vegetables

Can of cream soup

Directions

Make a "mess of rice" main dish. Use rice (or leftover noodles) to make a stove top dinner with whatever's handy. Start by browning an onion and meat if you have any. A single boneless breast or thigh will stretch to feed a family of four with this method. Sprinkle onion with garlic powder, parsley (or some other mild seasoning of your choice), salt, and pepper as desired. Drop in between a half and whole cup frozen diced vegetables. Stir to thaw. Lower heat and add a thickening agent such as a can of cream of mushroom, cream of tomato, cream of chicken, or cream of celery soup. Throw in your leftover rice or other starch and stir to mix. Heat through and serve. You can also throw in a handful of grated cheddar, jack or mozzarella cheese and stir to melt.

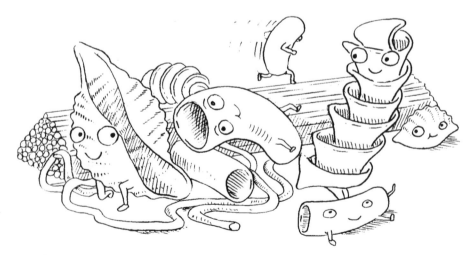

Lotsa Pasta

Probably the most common quick dinner around our house is organized around pasta.

Quick Veggie Pasta

Ingredients

Chopped onion

Minced garlic

Oil

Chopped vegetables

Italian seasoning blend

Cooked pasta

Grated Parmesan cheese

Directions

With an odd assortment of vegetables, an onion, a garlic clove and maybe meat, dinner is on the table in less than ten minutes. Put your pasta on to cook. In a skillet, add chopped onion and some garlic to one or two tablespoons olive oil and sauté over medium high heat. Stir until the onion is soft. Chop a tomato, mushrooms, zucchini, broccoli, eggplant, spinach, celery or whatever you have into the pan and stir. Sprinkle with Italian seasoning, flaked oregano or parsley, rosemary, basil leaves, sun-dried tomato bits or whatever seasoning you like. Add a dribble of water or white wine if the pan dries out. If you want to add meat, add it now although I usually use these dinners as vegetarian nights because I like it better that way. Sprinkle with salt and pepper and turn off heat. When pasta is done, drain it and add it to your vegetables. Toss pasta and vegetables and sprinkle generously with grated Parmesan. Crumbled feta cheese also works well. Another way to go is to sprinkle grated mozzarella over the pasta and veggies and cover for a few minutes with the heat off to melt the cheese. Then serve.

* Easier yet and satisfying with salad and vegetables on the side is simply to toss hot pasta with butter or margarine and sprinkle with salt, pepper, and grated Parmesan cheese. Kids love this.

Dressed Pasta

Ingredients

Onion

Meat

Non-creamy salad dressing such as French, Italian, Sweet and Tangy (page 106)

Cooked pasta

Directions

Use non-creamy salad dressing to create a quick pasta sauce with browned meat and onion. Brown ground turkey or beef with a chopped onion while pasta is cooking. Add a cup or so of your favorite non-creamy dressing. Mix it into the meat mixture and toss with hot pasta. This dinner is a real quick fix and it also works with sautéed vegetables and no meat.

Mac and Cheese

Ingredients

2-3 c cooked pasta elbows, bowties or corkscrews

1 T butter

1 tomato, chopped

2 c grated cheddar or longhorn cheese

Italian seasoning blend

Directions

Put hot pasta elbows in a microwave safe pan or bowl, toss with a tablespoon of butter, a chopped tomato and cheese. Add more cheese if you like. Put this into the microwave on high for a minute or two, stir and microwave again if cheese is not fully melted. Sprinkle with Italian seasoning blend or salt and pepper and serve immediately so cheese is hot when enjoyed. If you prefer, you can bake it in the oven at 400° for 10 minutes or so.

Mac and Cheese with Tuna

Ingredients

1 box macaroni and cheese dinner

1 12-oz can tuna, drained

2-3 T mayonnaise-style salad dressing (such as Miracle Whip®)

Directions

You either love or hate this casserole-style macaroni and cheese dish. My kids have always considered it a treat; maybe yours will, too. Make up the stovetop mac-and-cheese. While the pasta is cooking, mix a large can of drained tuna with salad dressing. Press this into the bottom of a pie tin or cake dish. Cover with the stove top macaroni and cheese and bake in the oven at 400° for 10 or 15 minutes. Sounds weird, but it's a great quick dinner for those who like it. You can add thawed peas to the macaroni and cheese if you like.

Spread It on Bread

If you have a focaccia bread, prebaked pizza shell, baguette, or even sliced sourdough, French or Italian bread, dinner is probably not far away. (The only bread I don't bother doing this with is wheat bread because I don't like it.) These dinner ideas also make great party food ideas for kids, teens and adults alike.

Southwestern Feast

Spread bread with salsa (or, in a pinch, tomato sauce sprinkled with garlic powder and cumin) and top with any or all of the following: chopped green onions, tomatoes, bell pepper, cilantro and corn. Then drain a small can of kidney, black or pinto beans and sprinkle them on the bread. Top with grated jack or cheddar cheese and broil until cheese is melted or bake at 425° for about 15-20 minutes or until cheese is melted.

Hamburger Heaven

Brown a patty or two of ground beef or ground turkey and break it up with a fork. Season it with garlic powder, salt and pepper. On your bread, spread tomato or pizza sauce. In a pinch, you can spread a thin layer of catsup. Sprinkle on your ground beef. Then add thin slices of onion or chopped green onion, dill or sweet pickles, and an optional chopped tomato. Top with grated cheddar cheese and bake or broil as you would pizza. This one is lots of fun and a great surprise party food.

Italian Adventure

This is just a reminder that Italian pizza can be jazzed up to be a complete meal. Spread pizza or marinara sauce on bread. On it place chopped green onions, diced broccoli tips, mushrooms, bell pepper, zucchini and whatever other vegetable seems right. Add your mozzarella and a sprinkle of pasta seasoning and bake for a great dinner with your veggies already on board. Sometimes when the vegetables are hidden, they go down without kids even noticing them. Diced fresh basil leaves make this pizza a real taste treat.

Veggie Treat

Mix two parts mayonnaise and one and a half parts grated Parmesan cheese with a generous sprinkle of garlic powder. Spread on bread or pizza-style bread. Top with diced fresh veggies that cook quickly such as mushrooms, eggplant, zucchini, onion, tomato, and artichoke hearts. Bake for twenty minutes or so at 425° as you would any pizza. If you reverse the order of these ingredients on the bread, i.e., put the vegetables on first and then spread with the mayo/Parmesan mixture, you can broil it for a few minutes until the sauce is bubbly and golden brown and then serve. Alternately, sauté the vegetables first and then sprinkle them on the bread. Top with grated mozzarella and broil for a couple minutes to melt cheese.

Indoor Barbeque

Spread barbeque sauce on bread. Brown onions and red bell pepper slices in vegetable oil together with a single boneless chicken breast or thigh. Cut the meat up as it cooks. Alternately, use a piece of leftover chicken (grilled meat tastes best but any will do) and cut it into small pieces. Spread the onions, peppers and meat over the barbeque sauce. Top with grated jack cheese and bake or broil. This pizza bread tastes best with lots of browned onions.

Potato Mash

If you have a box of potato flakes or buds, can you pull a dinner out of it? Of course. One way is a quick feast from the British Isles.

Irish Potatoes

Ingredients
Instant mashed potatoes

Shredded cabbage

Directions
Make mashed potatoes according to package directions. To feed 4, make about 3 cups of potatoes. If you have cabbage, chop it thinly like coleslaw. Better yet, keep a bag of coleslaw in the fridge. It lasts a long time and a handful of fresh shredded cabbage is a great addition to any stir fry or salad you make. Grab a couple of handfuls of cabbage from a bag of coleslaw and steam it stovetop or in the microwave while you prepare the mashed potatoes. Drain your limp cabbage and mix it into your finished mashed potatoes with salt and pepper to taste. Serve a large dollop of this Irish mashed potatoes and cabbage (which is called colcannon in Ireland) with a pat of butter melting on the top. Kids in Ireland have loved it for generations and kids elsewhere seem to respond well, too. To turn this dish into a variation of English "bubble and squeak," add to your colcannon a handful of cooked leftover meat cut up into small pieces. Stir well and serve. Dinner is ready in 10 minutes. With a green or fruit salad on the side, you have everything you need.

Kielbasa and Potatoes

Ingredients

Instant mashed potatoes

Frozen vegetables

Kielbasa (Polish sausage), sliced

Grated cheddar cheese

Directions

For a quick potluck favorite, prepare mashed potatoes according to package directions and mix with thawed frozen peas and carrots, a sliced Polish sausage (kielbasa), and a handful or two of grated cheddar cheese. Bake in the oven at 400° until the cheese is melted—about 15 to 20 minutes. This one is ready in less than a half hour and is usually a big hit. The active prep time takes less than 10 minutes.

Mashed Salad

On a salad note, leftover mashed potatoes can be turned into a midwestern favorite—mashed potato salad. You make it the same way you would potato salad except that you don't need to boil and slice all those potatoes. Mix into your mashed potatoes either mayonnaise or mayonnaise-style salad dressing with a dollop of pickle relish. Squirt in a small amount of mustard. Then add chopped celery, green onion, bell pepper, hard boiled egg and whatever else appeals to you. If you like it tangier, splash in a little vinegar or add more pickle relish or dressing. Sprinkle with salt and pepper. Mix it up well and refrigerate. Serve cold.

For the Grill or the Oven

You can make a quick meal on the grill or in the oven with fish, chicken, meat or veggies. While a great steak can be made in minutes with just a sprinkle of garlic powder, salt and pepper, sauces and marinades add some pizzazz to most grilled or oven-baked meats. Sauces can be brushed onto meat right before cooking. They require only a few ingredients and go together in just a few minutes. Marinades are quick to make, too. You can soak the meat over night in the marinade or you can coat and bake just like the sauces. Two sauces in the main sections of this book that work well as marinades with any main dish protein are the teriyaki sauce found under Teriyaki Whatever (page

86) and the tangy soy sauce under Tangy Chicken Wings (page 39). Several other quick, tasty marinades follow.

Lemony Paprika Sauce (for chicken or white fish)

Ingredients

3 T olive oil

2 T lemon juice (about half a lemon)

1 T paprika

1 t garlic powder

1/2 t salt

Directions

Whisk the ingredients together and brush on before grilling or oven baking.

Fruity Ginger Sauce

Ingredients

1 c peach preserves

3 T apple cider vinegar

2 T fresh ginger, peeled and diced or 1 t ground ginger

Directions

Mix ingredients and brush onto chicken or pork. You can substitute apricot preserves if you choose.

Zip-Zing Sauce

Ingredients

1 part apple cider or red wine vinegar

1 part chili sauce or catsup

Directions

Whisk equal parts of these two ingredients together to make a great grilling sauce for any meat. If you like a spicy hot sauce, mix the vinegar with a hot chili sauce. If you like food tangy, but not hot, simply mix vinegar with catsup. This sauce is great baked into the meat, but may be a little strong for dipping after the meat is done.

Zesty BBQ Sauce

Ingredients

1 c catsup

1/2 c apple cider vinegar

1/2 c brown sugar, packed

1 t prepared mustard

1 T Worcestershire sauce

1 t garlic powder

Directions

Mix all ingredients, coat meat and bake or grill. In the middle of winter when it has been months since you have grilled, a fast dinner that satisfies can be made by brushing barbeque sauce onto boneless chicken and baking it while you get the salad and other fixings ready. The preparation time is hardly five minutes and the baking time for boneless meat is often less than 30 minutes, depending upon the cut of meat baked.

Balsamic Butter Sauce

Ingredients

2 T balsamic vinegar

4 T butter, melted

Directions

Whisk vinegar into butter and brush onto shrimp, scallops and other shellfish right off the grill. This sauce can also be used on grilled vegetables.

Lemon-Rosemary Marinade (for chicken and fish)

1/8 c lemon juice

2 T each red wine vinegar and olive oil

1 t each garlic powder, sugar, and fresh diced rosemary leaves

1/2 t each salt and pepper

Orange Herb Marinade (for beef and chicken)

1/4 c orange juice

2 T red wine vinegar

1 T vegetable oil

1 t each garlic powder and paprika

1/2 t salt

1/8 t pepper

Tropical Marinade (especially good with chicken, fish, or pork)

1/2 c pineapple juice

1/8 c apple cider vinegar

2 T each honey, catsup, and soy sauce

1 t each garlic powder and ground ginger

Garlic Rub

Try a dry spice rub for a quick meat entrée. Rub all sides of any meat and then grill, bake or broil.

Ingredients

1 t each garlic powder, onion powder, and ground paprika

1/2 t each salt and ground black pepper

* For a spicer rub, reduce paprika to 1/2 teaspoon and add 1/2 teaspoon chili powder. For a rub that is great on pork, try this Scandanavian-style rub.

1 t each ground allspice and ground black pepper

1/2 t salt

Some of This, Some of That

Stir Fry Dinner

Ready in 15 minutes, healthy, inexpensive—these are some of the best reasons to make quick stir fry dinners and you don't need a recipe. Begin by checking your pantry for some basic ingredients.

Ingredients

Chopped onion

Garlic (clove or powder)

Ginger (root or powder)

Chopped vegetables

Oil

Soy Sauce

Directions

Chop the veggies into small pieces. This takes about five minutes. Great veggies to use are broccoli, carrots, zucchini, green beans, fresh spinach, bean sprouts, cabbage and bell pepper, to name a few. Thawed frozen succotash, corn and other veggies can also be added. Start cooking with 1 to 2 tablespoons hot vegetable oil in a skillet. Put in chopped onion and minced garlic and move it quickly around the pan. (If you use garlic powder instead of fresh garlic, wait to add it with vegetables.) Next, add any non-leafy, non-sprout vegetables you have—that is, your broccoli, celery, zucchini, and/or green beans. Move these around until they turn bright green. This is only a minute or two unless they are chopped into large pieces. Then add your leafy and sprout veggies and keep them moving. These need only a minute or less in the hot oil. Sprinkle with soy sauce as you stir and add a few splashes of sesame oil, if you have it. This is fine just as it is over white rice.

* If you have fresh ginger, mince it and add it with the garlic when you first begin your stir fry as it smells and tastes wonderful.

* To add meat to your stir fry, add cooked meat at the end with leafy veggies. Add uncooked meat in one-inch pieces at the beginning with the onion. You can also add protein with an egg, nuts, or tofu squares. To add an egg, make a space in the side of your pan. Drizzle in a little oil, drop on the egg and scramble very quickly over high heat. When the egg is cooked, mix it into the rest of the vegetables.

Sauté and Salad Dressing

When I don't know what to make and I run into boneless chicken, calamari rings, salad shrimp or fish fillets in the freezer, I know I can do dinner in 10 minutes with a little oil, onions and salad dressing. Begin the thawing process in the microwave. I begin defrosting chicken by turning the microwave on high for 3 or 4 minutes. For seafood, use much shorter increments of time or the defrost button. The meat or seafood doesn't need to be fully thawed for its stove-top experience, just softened up some.

Put some oil and chopped onion in the pan and sauté until the onion is soft. Then add your meat. As it begins to cook and you flip it over, break it into pieces in the pan with a knife and fork to speed the cooking process. Drizzle your favorite non-creamy dressing over the meat. Good dressing choices to have handy in the fridge are red wine vinaigrette, spicy French, spicy red California-style dressing, Russian or Italian. Turn the heat down to medium low and cover until meat is done. Serve with quick rice or noodles.

Fajita Fever

If chicken, pork, ground beef or beef strips are what your refrigerator reveals, you might go a little different direction. Sauté the meat, an onion, and a clove of garlic, minced, in oil. Add chopped tomato, bell pepper or zucchini if you have them. Season with taco seasoning or oregano, cumin, garlic powder, paprika, chili powder, salt, and pepper. Serve with rice or, fold the results into a tortilla. There are few dinners quicker than stove top fajitas. It's basically a stir fry, southwestern style.

* This same cooking method can be used with thawed frozen seafood blends that include white fish, calamari rings, scallops and shrimp. Thaw the fish in water so the excess liquid is gone before you begin cooking. Then brown an onion with minced garlic. Add chopped tomato or bell pepper as you choose and your fish chunks. Season as they cook with ground cumin, fresh cilantro leaves, paprika and/or chili powder. You may lower heat, cover, and let fish steam to cook through. When fish is done, serve with flour tortillas. Fill tortillas with fish mixture and refried beans topped with fresh chopped lettuce, tomato, cilantro, grated jack cheese, sour cream, salsa verde or whatever Tex-Mex garnishes you like.

Before the Meal

Sometimes around holidays or at other times of the year it's nice to have handy some very easy appetizers to throw on when company calls or just to make a dinner with family more festive. Here are a couple of the ideas you probably knew, but may have forgotten.

Dressed Cream Cheese

If you have a block of cream cheese, you probably have an appetizer. Place cream cheese on a plate and top with any of the following for a quick, tasty treat:

Mild or hot pepper jelly

Wine Jelly

Salsa

Chutney

Chili Sauce with salad shrimp

Raspberry jam

Serve raspberry-topped cheese with water crackers for best results. Otherwise, serve this appetizer with thin wheat crackers, stone ground wheats, melba toasts, or any other crackers you like.

Finger Salad

A quick way to create an elegant meal starter is to turn salad into something more fun. Put out three or four small bowls of favorite salad dressings. Serve with baby lettuce or finger size pieces of romaine and other lettuce that diners dip into dressings of their choice. This can even be done with a bag of mixed greens which are usually cut into pieces rather large for salad, but great for dipping. To serve elegantly, line a bowl with large leaves of romaine and fill with a bag of mixed specialty greens. Surround bowl with salad dressings for dipping. This takes no time but makes salad great fun for family or entertaining.

Mediterranean Starter

An elegant way to begin a meal that takes no time is to cut a baguette into rounds or a large French or Italian loaf into bite size pieces. Serve with one or both of these dipping sauces—a small bowl of good olive oil and a small bowl of your favorite marinara sauce. A flavored oil is nice if you have it. If not, you can flavor your own by adding Italian seasoning, rosemary and crushed garlic, or parsley and oregano flakes to plain olive oil. A great dipping alternative to marinara sauce is fresh bruschetta sauce (page 32).

When it comes to getting food on the table quickly, what is fast and easy for me is not necessarily fast and easy for you. I have friends who think that tacos with leftover whatever are a great quick dinner, but for me they are torture because of all the little pieces and things that go into them. It's worth it, though, to try some of these "cook as you are ideas." Come back to this section whenever you don't know what to put on the table or are feeling that mealtime is monotonous. Your family might even look forward to leftovers.

Extra Easy Appetizers

It's quick and easy to make mouth-watering appetizers for company or a potluck—so quick and easy you'll want to make some just for the family.

Brie with Pecans

Ingredients
2 T butter

1/3 c brown sugar (packed down)

Wedge of Brie (about .5 to .7 lb)

1/2 c pecans

Dash cinnamon

Water crackers

Directions
Cut the skin off the top of the Brie. In a skillet, melt butter and add brown sugar. Stir to melt and add pecans and cinnamon. Place Brie in pan suitable for broiling and spoon melted mixture over it. Broil for several minutes, watching carefully to avoid burning. Serve immediately with water crackers. Serves 4.

Preparation Time: less than 10 minutes

*   This one sounds strange but it's a winner with everyone. It seems to garner rave reviews even when you think it didn't turn out quite right. I made it for years without being sure what the proportions were and there was never any left no matter how it turned out.

*   This recipe also works nicely as a dessert served alongside fresh fruit.

Chutney Dip

Ingredients

1 c sour cream or plain yogurt

1 T Major Grey's chutney

1 T chopped chives

Crackers, melba toasts and fresh vegetables

Directions

Chop up any large pieces of fruit in the chutney. Mix together with sour cream and chives. Serve with water crackers, wheat crackers, melba toasts or fresh vegetables.

Preparation Time: under 5 minutes

* For the chutney dip, you can delete the chives if you don't have them. Also, the recipe works fine with light sour cream.

* You can turn this recipe into a different type of dip by substituting your favorite salsa for the chutney. You may need to add more salsa for the taste you like. Serve with crackers, chips or vegetables.

* Turn this recipe into a fresh fruit dip by substituting orange marmalade, strawberry or raspberry preserves for the chutney and deleting the chives.

Baguette and Bruschetta

Ingredients

3 tomatoes, diced or chopped

6 large fresh basil leaves, diced

1-2 t crushed garlic

1 T olive oil

1/4 t salt

1/4 t pepper

1 t balsamic vinegar

Pinch sugar

Baguette

Directions

Dice tomatoes into bowl. Drain off excess juice. Dice basil. Add basil and all remaining ingredients and stir. Serve with whole baguette. Cut or tear and dip into sauce. Or, spoon bruschetta onto baguette slices.

Preparation Time: 5-10 minutes

*   For best results, use roma tomatoes.

*   To make dicing fresh basil easy, lay the leaves on top of each other and roll tightly. Make one lengthwise cut and then mince by cutting crosswise.

*   The amount of garlic you use depends upon what you like. Two teaspoons tastes great.

Guacamole Pronto

Ingredients

4 medium avocados, mashed

1/2 t garlic powder

Juice of 1/2 lemon

1/4 c mild chunky salsa

Directions

Mash avocados with potato masher. Add remaining ingredients and stir until well mixed. Makes 1 to 1-1/2 cups guacamole.

Preparation Time: less than 5 minutes

* Serve with tortilla chips or use as a sauce for quesadillas or on hamburgers.

* If you like a richer guacamole, add two tablespoons sour cream or plain yogurt and 2 tablespoons mayonnaise.

Chili and Chips

Ingredients

1 16-oz can no-bean chili

8 oz cream cheese

Tortilla chips

Directions

Heat chili in saucepan over medium heat. As chili gets warm, cut cream cheese chunks into it. Stir constantly to melt cream cheese. When cream cheese is melted, serve immediately with tortilla chips.

Preparation Time: 5 minutes

Hot Tangy Bean Dip

Ingredients

1 16-oz can refried beans

1/3 c sour cream

1/2 c cheddar cheese, grated

Diced green onions

Tortilla chips

Directions

Preheat oven to 400°. In an ovenproof serving dish, mix first three ingredients together well and heat until cheese is melted, about 10 to 15 minutes. Sprinkle with diced green onion and serve with tortilla chips.

Preparation Time: working time 5 minutes/baking time 15 minutes

*   To serve this dish as a side of refried beans, reduce the sour cream to 1/4 cup. This dip makes a great Tex-Mex side dish alongside Spanish rice.

Cheesy Shrimp Dip

Ingredients

1 c cooked salad-size shrimp, defrosted

8 oz cream cheese

1 green onion, diced

Directions

Mix all ingredients together and place in small baking dish. Bake at 350° for about 20 minutes. Serve with crackers, bread chunks or vegetables.

Preparation Time: 5 minutes working time/20 minutes baking time

*   You can shorten the baking time of this dip by heating it in the microwave. Cook at 30-second intervals on high and stir until warmed to your satisfaction.

Tortilla Roll-Ups

Ingredients

1/2 10-oz pkg frozen chopped spinach, thawed

8 oz cream cheese, softened

2-3 T mayonnaise

1 green onion, diced

1 t garlic powder

1/4 t paprika

4 soft-taco size flour tortillas

Directions

Mix spinach (press as much water out of it as possible), cream cheese, mayonnaise, onion, paprika and garlic powder. Cut 1/2 inch off two opposite sides of each tortilla. Spread a quarter of spinach mixture over each tortilla. Roll tightly and cut into 1/2-inch pieces (about 6 to 7 pieces per tortilla). Makes about 24 pieces.

Preparation Time: 15 minutes

* You can substitute 1/2 teaspoon onion powder for the diced green onion and the results are still good. You can also add a dash of cayenne.

* This mixture can also be turned into a dip for fresh vegetables and chips by adding 2 tablespoons sour cream and 2 tablespoons mayonnaise.

* Make a quick spinach dip with your remaining half box of spinach. Mix your squeezed-out spinach with 1 8-ounce container sour cream, 1/2 cup mayonnaise and some or all of a package of onion soup mix, depending upon taste preferences. You can add chopped sliced water chestnuts to this if you like your dip crunchy. Serve with vegetables and bread chunks.

* If you like a good pickle, another cream cheese roll-up appetizer you might like is made like this: On a slice of thin sandwich-style ham, spread (somewhat generously) cream cheese. Roll this around a crisp, dill pickle. Slice into 1/4-inch thick medallions and serve. Not only is this a tasty snack, but it is visually attractive, too.

Tex-Mex Squares

Ingredients

4 c cheddar or longhorn cheese, grated

1 4-oz can diced green chiles

6 eggs

1/2 t garlic powder

1/2 t ground cumin

Directions

Preheat oven to 350°. Grease a 7 by 10 inch baking dish with non-stick cooking spray. Mix all ingredients in a bowl and pour into pan. Bake for 30 minutes or until knife inserted in the center comes out clean. Let cool for 15 minutes and cut into one-inch squares. Makes about 70 pieces.

Preparation Time: 5 minutes working time/45 minutes baking and cooling time

Spinach Bake

Ingredients

1 10-oz pkg frozen chopped spinach, thawed

Garlic powder

3/4 c mayonnaise

1/4 c grated Parmesan cheese

Directions

Preheat oven to 350°. Press as much water out of spinach as possible. Spread in the bottom of an 8-inch square baking dish. Sprinkle generously with garlic powder. Spread mayonnaise on spinach and sprinkle with Parmesan cheese. Bake until slightly golden and bubbly. Serve with wheat crackers or French bread medallions.

Preparation Time: 5 minutes working time/15-20 minutes baking time

*   This appetizer can also be made by lining the bottom of the pan with chopped artichoke hearts instead of spinach.

*   Another way to use this recipe idea is to simply mix 1/2 cup mayonnaise and 1/3 cup Parmesan with 1/2 teaspoon garlic powder and a teaspoon of minced chives. Spread this mixture on bite-size melba or other dry toasts. Broil until lightly browned and serve immediately. They are very tasty and quick.

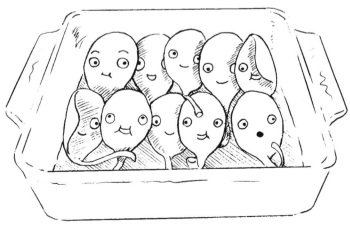

Stuffed Mushrooms

Ingredients

24 small fresh mushroom caps, stems removed

4 oz cream cheese

1/4 c finely grated Parmesan cheese

1 t diced chives

1/4 t garlic powder

Directions

Mix cream cheese, Parmesan cheese, chives, and garlic powder. Press by the teaspoonful into mushroom caps. Broil until lightly browned on top. Serve immediately.

Preparation Time: less than 10 minutes working time/less than 5 minutes baking time

*   As an alternate filling that takes a bit more time, dice mushroom stems and add them to your filling.

Tangy Chicken Wings

Ingredients
2 lbs chicken wingettes

1/2 c soy sauce

1/2 c sugar

1/4 c red wine vinegar

1/2 t garlic powder

Directions
Preheat oven to 375°. Place chicken wings in a 9 by 13 inch baking dish. Mix marinade and pour over them. Bake for about 45 minutes. Turn once during baking.

Preparation Time: 5 minutes working time/45 minutes baking time

* These wings can be made ahead and reheated by placing in oven for 10 minutes at 400°.

* You can marinate wings in sauce over night for better flavor, but they taste great even when made on the run.

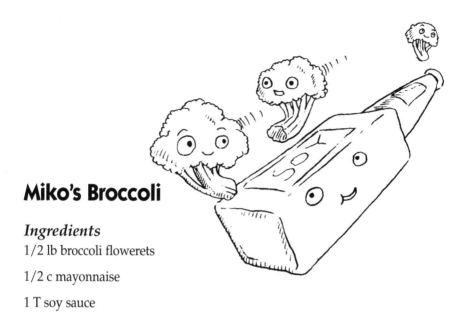

Miko's Broccoli

Ingredients

1/2 lb broccoli flowerets

1/2 c mayonnaise

1 T soy sauce

Directions

Steam broccoli flowerets stovetop or in microwave. (In microwave, put them in covered container with 1/4 cup water for 2 minutes on high. Leave covered as they cool.)

Mix mayonnaise and soy sauce. Put in small bowl and serve with cooled broccoli which is dipped into the sauce.

Preparation Time: 5 minutes

*   This one may sound a little strange, but it was introduced to me by my college roommate who was from Japan. People can't figure out what the dip is but go back for more every time.

*   A different twist on this appetizer is to serve cooled broccoli with a dipping sauce of 2 parts balsamic vinegar and 1 part Dijon mustard.

Sausage Bites

Ingredients

1/2 lb bulk or patty breakfast sausage

1 1/4 c biscuit mix such as Bisquik®

1 c grated cheddar cheese

1/4 t chili powder or cracked black pepper

Directions

Preheat oven to 350°. Mix sausage with biscuit mix. When well mixed, add in cheese and spice. Mix well and form into balls smaller than 1 inch. Bake on ungreased cookie sheet for 20 minutes or until golden. Makes about 48.

Preparation Time: 10-15 minutes working time/20 minutes baking time

*   These appetizers can also be made with cayenne pepper, but you might want to cut the amount of pepper suggested in half unless you like your food very hot.

*   These can be served alone warm or with Dijon mustard as a dipping sauce. Dijon mustard with a little honey also makes a good dipping sauce.

*   These can be made ahead, baked and frozen. To reheat, thaw and bake at 300° for about 10 minutes.

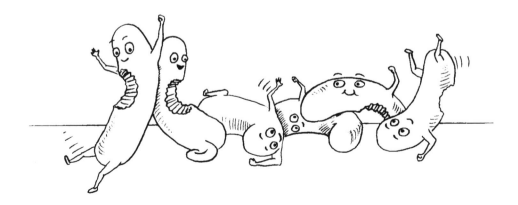

Italian Pull-Apart Bread

Ingredients
1 10-biscuit roll refrigerated buttermilk biscuits

Olive oil

Garlic powder

Italian seasoning blend

Sun-dried tomato bits

Grated Parmesan cheese

Grated mozzarella cheese

Directions
Preheat oven to 375°. Grease cookie sheet with non-stick cooking spray. Lay out biscuits in a circle/oval shape and press edges slightly together. Brush biscuits with olive oil. Sprinkle with remaining ingredients, ending with cheeses. Bake for about 15 minutes. Serve immediately.

Preparation Time: 5 minutes working time/15 minutes baking time

*   This bread can be reheated in the microwave in a sealed plastic bag with a few drops of water by heating it on high for 30 seconds.

*   You can save time making this bread by using the same ingredients on an unsliced loaf of French or Italian bread cut in half the long way. Broil the finished bread to melt cheese. Cut in strips to serve.

*   A Tex-Mex version of the pull-apart bread is as follows: Brush prepared biscuits with olive oil. Sprinkle with garlic powder, ground cumin, 4-oz drained diced green chiles, chopped green onion, and grated jack or cheddar cheese. Bake at 375° for 15 minutes.

*   Another quick biscuit appetizer is blue cheese bites. Quarter the refrigerated biscuits. Melt about 1/3 stick of butter with 3 to 4 tablespoons crumbled blue or Gorgonzola cheese. Roll the biscuits in the butter mixture, sprinkle with fresh cracked black pepper, and bake at 400° until golden brown (about 10 minutes). Stir once while baking. Serve immediately.

*   For a pull-apart breakfast treat, quarter biscuits, roll them in melted butter and cinnamon sugar, and bake at 400° until golden brown (about 10 minutes).

Onion Foccacia

Ingredients

1 large sweet onion, sliced thin

2 cloves garlic, minced

1/4 t crushed thyme

2 T olive oil

1 large (about 10-inch) ready-made, baked pizza crust such as Boboli®

1 c grated Parmesan or Gruyère cheese

Directions

Sauté onions, garlic and thyme in olive oil until onions are translucent. Arrange them on the pizza crust. Sprinkle with cheese and a little more thyme. Broil for several minutes until cheese melts and is just golden. Cut into thin slices and serve warm.

Preparation Time: less than 10 minutes

* You can use other cheeses if you choose such as grated mozzarella or provolone.

* If you don't have thyme, you can substitute tarragon or rosemary for a different taste treat.

Crusty Bread with Basil Butter

Ingredients
1 loaf crusty French bread

2 T butter or margarine, melted (1/4 stick)

1 t crushed garlic or garlic powder

1/4 c diced fresh basil leaves

Directions
Preheat oven to 375°. Split loaf in half lengthwise. Melt butter in microwave with garlic. Dice basil leaves and add to melted butter mixture. Paint butter mixture on both halves of loaf. Wrap in heavy duty foil or two layers foil and bake for about ten minutes.

Preparation Time: less than 5 minutes working time/10 minutes baking time

*   This one also works nicely with fresh parsley or fresh rosemary.

Green Chili Quesadillas

Ingredients
2 c grated cheddar cheese

2 green onions, chopped

1 4-oz can diced green chiles

6 soft taco-size flour tortillas

Directions
Mix first three ingredients in a bowl. Spread evenly onto three tortillas. Place under broiler until cheese is melted—about 3 to 4 minutes, depending upon your broiler. Remove from broiler and press three remaining tortillas on top of each cooked tortilla. Cut each into six pieces.

Preparation Time: less than 10 minutes

*   Serve with sour cream, salsa, picante sauce and/or guacamole (page 33).

Almonds Paprika

Ingredients

1 lb raw almonds

2 t olive oil

1 t garlic powder

1 t onion powder

1/2 t paprika

1/2 t chili powder

1/4 t salt

Directions

Heat olive oil in large skillet over medium high heat. Add almonds and stir to coat with oil. Continue stirring constantly for 3 to 5 minutes until almonds are toasted. Remove from heat. While almonds cool, mix seasonings together. Sprinkle over almonds and stir until seasoning evenly coats nuts.

Preparation Time: less than 10 minutes.

* These savory nuts are a great offering as an appetizer. They are quick, easy and can be made ahead eliminating the last minute heating and fussing of other appetizers.

* This recipe is only lightly salted. You can add more salt to taste after you finish tossing the original seasonings.

* These nuts make a nice holiday or hostess gift.

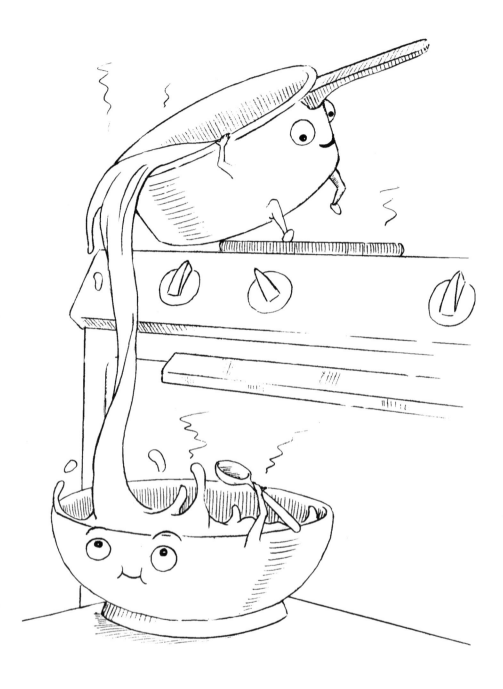

Simple Soups

A tasty soup starts off any dinner right, and a hearty soup makes a great whole meal. And if you think that canned soup is the only quick soup you are in for a surprise.

Spanish-Style Seafood Soup

Ingredients
2 T olive oil

1 onion, chopped

2 tomatoes, chopped

2 cloves garlic, minced or 1 t crushed garlic

2 cups fresh mussels, scrubbed and rinsed or 2 cups mixed frozen seafood such as calamari rings, small scallops and/or cooked shrimp

1 cup cooked rice

2 T chopped prosciutto, serrano-style ham or other smoked ham or cooked bacon

1 t salt

1 T parsley

2 T sherry or wine

Directions
Sauté onion, garlic, and tomatoes in oil while you thaw frozen seafood in microwave. Add parsley, salt, and ham and stir. Add six cups water, sherry, and rice. Bring to a boil, add seafood, and turn heat low to simmer for a few minutes—until mussels open or seafood is fully cooked.

Preparation Time: 15 minutes

* This is a great way to use up leftover rice. If you do not have leftover rice, throw in a 1/2 to 3/4 cup minute-style rice. If you use minute-style rice, you need to simmer it a few minutes to insure that the rice is cooked.

Side by Side
Served with crusty bread or onion foccacia (page 43). Or, try it with crusty bread with basil butter (page 44). You can substitute fresh cilantro or parsley for the basil. A lightly dressed green salad goes well with this dish. Try a vinaigrette or other non-creamy salad dressing for your greens.

Tortilla Soup

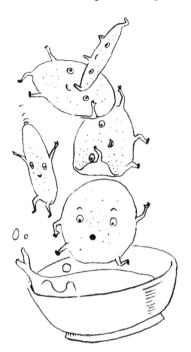

Ingredients

1/2 lb ground turkey

1 clove garlic, minced

1 onion, chopped

1 pkg enchilada sauce seasoning

1 large can (1 lb 12 oz) crushed tomatoes

1 15-oz can pinto beans, drained

1 15-oz can black beans, drained

1 15-oz can kernel corn, drained

2 c water

2 c crushed tortilla chips

Directions

Brown turkey with garlic and onion in soup pot. Add enchilada seasoning and mix well. Add remaining ingredients and bring to a boil. If you want a thinner soup, just add more water. Reduce heat and simmer until ready to serve. When serving, top each bowl with grated cheddar or jack cheese, dollop of sour cream, diced green onions and/or a tortilla chip. Serves 6-8.

Preparation Time: 10 minutes

*   You can add fresh chopped bell pepper, tomatoes or even a cup of frozen chopped spinach to this thick, hearty soup. If you add fresh vegetables, brown them with the meat and onion.

*   You can adjust the seasonings on this soup. Some spices that blend well with this soup are chili powder, cumin and paprika.

Side by Side

This soup makes a perfect quick dinner with a lightly dressed green salad or black bean salad (page 114) and cheese quesdadillas. Jazz up your quesadillas by topping the cheese with slices of ortega green chiles, onion, or bell pepper. Sweet red bell pepper is especially tasty. Serve quesadillas with your choice of sour cream, guacamole (page 33) and/or salsa.

Spicy Bean Soup

Ingredients

1 T olive oil

1 onion, chopped

1 t crushed garlic or 2 garlic cloves, minced

1 16-oz jar mild chunky salsa (about 2 cups)

1 16-oz can refried beans

1 14.5-oz can chicken broth (about 1 3/4 cups)

Directions

Sauté first three ingredients over high heat until onion is translucent. While these ingredients are cooking, mix remaining ingredients in a bowl. For quick mixing, use a potato masher. Add bean mixture to soup pot and bring to a boil. Serves 6 or more.

Preparation Time: less than 10 minutes

*   Garnish soup with grated cheddar cheese, fresh cilantro leaves and/or sour cream.

Side by Side

This soup makes a good dinner when accompanied by avocado and onion salad (page 113) or romaine with oranges and avocados (page 111). It can also be used as a first course in a Mexican dinner feast.

Southwestern Tomato Soup

Ingredients

1 green onion, chopped

2 14.5-oz cans chicken broth (about 3 1/2 cups)

2-3 c frozen corn kernels

1 24-oz thick and chunky salsa, mild (about 3 cups)

1 t garlic powder

2 T sugar

1 c milk (optional)

Directions

Heat broth and green onion over high heat. When the broth begins to boil, lower heat and add remaining ingredients. Stir and simmer for a few minutes. Serves 6-8.

Preparation Time: 5 to 10 minutes

* You can add diced bell pepper or 1 4-ounce can diced green chiles to this soup, if you like.

* Garnish with cilantro sprig, sour cream, grated hard Mexican cheese, cheddar or jack.

* To make a quick cold Mexican tomato soup like gazpacho, try this: Mix 1 diced, peeled cucumber, a chopped tomato, 1 or 2 diced green onions, and 2 tablespoons chopped fresh cilantro with a 16-ounce can V-8® vegetable juice and 1 cup salsa of your choice. Serve garnished with sour cream and a cilantro sprig. It's ready in 5 minutes and serves four. Refrigerate your salsa and juice before preparing so the soup is chilled when finished. Make it spicier with a dash of Tabasco.

Side by Side

Serve this soup with Mexican pull-apart bread (page 42—recipe notes) or green chili quesadillas (page 44).

Cheesy Potato Soup

Ingredients

1 T butter or margarine

1 stalk celery, minced

1 onion, chopped

1/2 carrot, grated

1 t parsley

4 c water

3 c potato flakes

1 14-oz can evaporated milk

1 c milk

8 oz processed American cheese, cut into chunks

Directions

Put water on to boil while you sauté celery, onion, carrots and parsley in butter. When water begins to boil, add potato flakes. Turn heat off and add all milk and cheese. Mix well. Add vegetables. Turn heat onto low and stir to melt cheese and mix in milk and vegetables. Use a potato masher to speed this process. Add salt and pepper to taste, if you choose.

Preparation Time: 15 minutes

*   Tarragon or thyme are seasonings that you can substitute for parsley in this soup.

*   If you like your soup thinner, add more milk a little at a time.

Side by Side

Serve this soup with fresh fruit or greens tossed with sweet and tangy dressing (page 106). Or, use the sweet and tangy dressing over shredded fresh cabbage, green onions, almonds and crushed ramen noodles. Steamed broccoli or green beans are also good on the side.

Cabbage and Kielbasa Stew

Ingredients
1 onion, chopped

2 T vegetable oil

1 8-oz bag coleslaw

1 kielbasa (Polish sausage) link, cut into 1/4-inch medallions

1/4 cup sun-dried tomato bits

Pepper to taste

Directions
Sauté onion in oil. Add coleslaw, 4 cups water, tomato bits and kielbasa. Cover and bring to a boil. Reduce heat and simmer for about 10 minutes. Pepper to taste. Salt only as needed as kielbasa releases a lot of flavor.

Preparation Time: 15 minutes

* If you do not have sun-dried tomato bits in your market, you can cut sun-dried tomatoes into pieces or break them up in the blender. They are a very versatile and useful seasoning to have handy in the kitchen.

* If you want a soup, add more water to the stew. If you want a thicker dish, cook the stew longer to reduce the broth.

Side by Side
If you make this soup as a thick stew with only a little juice, it is great served over mashed potatoes. It can also be served over rice. If you want to add a green salad on the side, either a vinaigrette-style or creamy dressing will serve you well.

Crazy No-Beet Borscht

Ingredients

2 10.5-oz cans beef broth (2 3/4 cups)

2 16-oz cans whole berry cranberry sauce

2 10.5-oz cans tomato soup

1 8-oz bag coleslaw

1 onion, chopped

Directions

Put beef broth and onion in soup pot. Bring to a boil and add coleslaw. Boil until slaw is very limp. Add cranberry sauce and tomato soup. Bring to a boil, lower heat and simmer until ready to serve. Serves 6 or more.

Preparation Time: less than 10 minutes

* Serve with a dollop of sour cream.

* This can be made into a meat soup by adding fajita-cut or stir-fry cut beef strips to your beef broth. Boil the beef with the cabbage.

Side by Side

This soup has a sweet-sour flavor. Serve it with steamed squash or green beans. Broccoli salad (page 119) or a green salad dressed with a Russian or 999 Island (page 108) dressing goes well with this soup. This is a slightly thick soup. You might enjoy it served over a bed of rice, couscous or kasha (cracked wheat starch).

Chinese Egg and Rice Soup

Ingredients

3 14-oz cans chicken broth (about 5 1/4 cups)

2-3 medallions of fresh ginger (optional)

1/2 teaspoon garlic powder

1 cup minute-style rice (or use cooked rice leftovers)

1 cup frozen peas

2 eggs, beaten

4 green onions

Directions

Put the broth and ginger in a large soup pot and bring to a boil. While broth heats, beat two eggs slightly and cut up onions. Lower heat and add garlic powder, rice and peas. While the soup simmers, gradually drizzle in the beaten egg while gently stirring the soup. The egg blooms and cooks immediately. Toss in the green onions and serve immediately. Serves 4-6.

Preparation Time: less than 10 minutes

*   If you don't have canned chicken broth, you can use bouillon powder and water or even salted water.

*   It helps in cooking the egg to have an extra hand because the egg "flowers" best in the hot water if drizzled over the tongs of a fork. Ask a kitchen helper to hold the fork or stir gently while you drizzle. Then, two of you share the fun of watching the egg cook before your eyes.

*   It is best to serve this soup immediately because the egg settles to the bottom if the soup sits on the stove for long. It still tastes fine, but it doesn't look as interesting.

*   You can add other vegetables to this soup if you choose. Good choices are julienned carrots, sliced mushrooms and corn.

Side by Side

This soup goes well with a side of fresh vegetables chopped, stir-fried and seasoned with a splash of soy sauce, garlic powder and ginger powder. Serve the vegetables over rice.

Japanese Noodle Soup

Ingredients
6 cups water

1/2 lb stir-fry beef strips

4 quarter-size medallions ginger

4 T soy sauce

1 pkg yakisoba noodles

1/2 c julienned carrot strips

1 c sliced mushrooms

1 c diced green onions

2 c fresh baby spinach

Directions
Brown beef strips for about a minute in soup pot over medium high heat to seal in juices. Add water and ginger and bring to a boil over high heat. Use slotted spoon to remove any foam that develops near the edge of the pot. Lower heat and cook until beef is done. This takes two or three minutes. Add carrot strips and soba noodles and cook for about one minute. Add mushrooms and soy sauce and cook for an additional minute. Add onion and spinach, remove from heat and serve immediately. Serves 6.

Preparation Time: 10 minutes

*   You may add other thinly sliced vegetables that you like along with or instead of the mushrooms. Good choices include celery, zucchini, and snow peas.

*   Cooked spaghetti or capellini noodles can be substituted for yakisoba noodles if they are not available in your local market. Just add the cooked spaghetti as you would the yakisoba noodles.

Side by Side
This soup goes well with a salad of greens, julienned carrots, sliced mushrooms and cucumbers. Sprinkle with toasted sesame seeds if you have them and toss with sweet and tangy salad dressing (page 106).

Smoked Turkey Soup

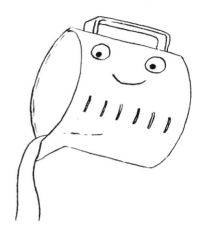

Ingredients

1 onion, chopped

8 c water

1/2 lb smoked turkey, chopped

1 16-oz bag coleslaw mix

1/2 t black pepper

1 t fresh thyme leaves

Directions

Brown onion over high heat. (No oil is necessary.) When onions are soft, add water, turkey, coleslaw mix, and seasonings. Bring to a boil. Then, lower heat and simmer for fifteen minutes. Salt to taste. Serves 6-8.

Preparation Time: 5 minutes working time/15 minutes cooking time

Side by Side

Serve this light soup with a side of beans or creamed corn and steamed rice. To prepare beans such as black, pink or butter beans, simply heat them right out of the can or sauté chopped onion and add the drained beans. Mash them slightly, season with garlic powder, and serve. Alternately, serve with a hearty bread such as crusty bread with basil butter (page 44) or onion foccacia (page 43).

Jumpin' John Soup

Ingredients

1 onion, chopped

1/2 lb ham, chopped

3 15-oz cans black-eyed peas, drained

1 c leftover rice (or cooked minute-style rice)

1 t garlic powder

1/4 t black pepper

1/2 t crushed thyme

4 c water

Directions

Brown onion in dry pan until translucent. Add rice, ham, peas, three cups water, and seasonings. Stir to blend well and heat. Mash beans slightly with a potato masher to thicken soup broth. If you are going to eat this soup as soon as it is warm, you may not need the fourth cup of water. If you are going to eat it later or the next day, add the last cup as the soup thickens as it sets. Serves 6-8.

Preparation Time: 10 minutes

*   This soup can also be made with cannellini (white kidney), navy or white beans.

*   This soup is a variation of a traditional southern bean and rice dish called Hoppin' John. Hoppin' John is a customary New Year's dish.

Side by Side

This hearty soup is best served with a light green salad or a sliced fruit or fruit salad accompaniment.

Onion Soup

Ingredients

1 large onion, chopped

2 T butter or margarine (1/4 stick)

2 garlic cloves, minced

2 14-oz cans ready-to-serve beef broth (about 3 1/2 cups)

2 c croutons

4 slices French bread, toasted

1 c grated Gruyère cheese or 4 slices Swiss cheese

Directions

Place 1/2 cup croutons in each of four oven-safe bowls. Slice four rounds of French bread about 1/2 to 1 inch thick. Grate Gruyère cheese. Sauté onion and garlic in butter. Add beef broth and heat through. Pour broth (dividing onions as evenly as possible) into the four bowls. Top with round of French bread and sprinkle with cheese. Broil for two to three minutes, or until cheese is melted and slightly browned at the edges.

Preparation Time: 15 minutes

* Large sweet onions are good for this recipe. If your onion is not large, use two onions. If you like lots of onion in your soup, chop and sauté two large onions.

* If you don't have Gruyère (which is the traditional cheese for this dish) or prefer not to invest in it as it is rather pricey, you can top the bread with a slice of Swiss cheese. Other cheese possibilities are grated Parmesan or jack cheese. Brown in the broiler but watch it carefully so it does not burn.

* While this soup makes a great meal starter, it also serves well as a quick main course with a salad when you don't have much in the house.

Side by Side

A salad of tossed romaine and baby spinach with diced fresh vegetables rounds out this soup nicely into a meal for the family. Toss the salad with sweet and tangy (page 106) or balsamic vinaigrette (page 107) dressing.

Tomato Florentine Soup

Ingredients

1 T olive oil

2 cloves garlic, minced

1 onion, chopped

1 c mushrooms, sliced

1 10-oz pkg frozen chopped spinach, thawed

1 28-oz can crushed tomatoes

2 T Italian seasoning blend

Salt and pepper to taste

Directions

Thaw spinach in microwave on high for 5 minutes. While spinach is thawing, sauté garlic, onions and mushrooms in oil over medium high heat until onions are soft. Add spinach, crushed tomatoes, Italian seasoning blend, 1 can water, salt, and pepper. Turn heat down to medium and simmer for 5 to 10 minutes.

Preparation Time: 15 minutes

* You can substitute two teaspoons crushed garlic from a jar to save time.

* You can add chopped sun-dried tomato along with seasoning blend.

* Change the vegetables in the sauté, if you like, to include bell pepper, fresh tomatoes, or zucchini.

* If you add salt and pepper, begin with 1/4 teaspoon salt and several generous twists of the pepper mill. You can garnish this soup with Parmesan cheese to serve.

* Add a teaspoon of sugar to bring out the flavors. This is a good trick to improve the flavor blending of many dishes.

Side by Side

Serve with crusty bread with basil butter (page 44) or onion foccacia (page 43) and a green salad or hot green vegetable.

Yam Soup

Ingredients

2 T butter

1 small onion, diced

3 c apple juice

2 29-oz cans yams, drained

1 t cumin

1 t salt

1/4 t pepper

1/8 t cinnamon

Directions

Brown onion in butter. Add yams and mash with potato masher. Add juice one cup at the time. Blend yams into juice. Add seasonings, stir and heat through. Garnish with a dollop of sour cream or plain yogurt and a sprig of parsley or cilantro. Serves 6.

Preparation Time: less than 15 minutes

* This is a hearty, thick dinner soup that blends sweet and tangy flavors. It is reminiscent of Indian food. It is a great addition to autumn and winter dinner parties.

Side by Side

Serve with cornbread, garlic bread or muffins along with a green salad. Romaine with oranges and avocados (page 111) offers a nice complement.

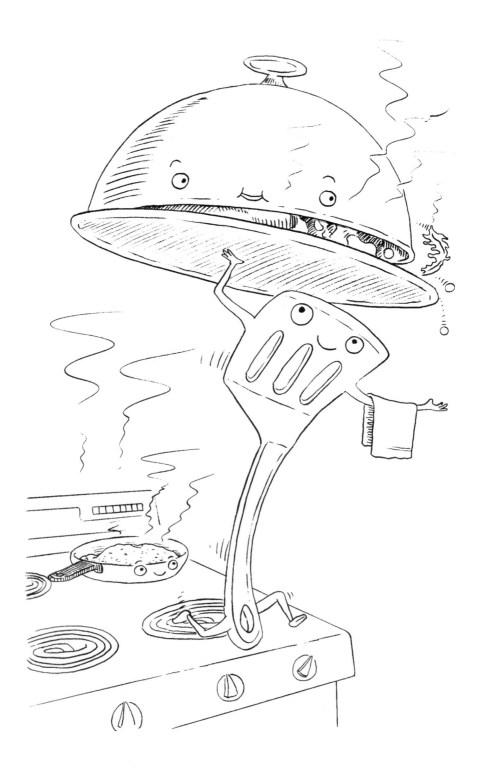

Made-in-Minutes Main Dishes

Here's a chance to vary your repertoire—without spending a lot of time or effort. And there's lots of variety for even the pickiest eaters in your family.

More➡

64~Made-in-Minutes Main Dishes

Turkey Cutlets—Picata Style

Ingredients
1 T vegetable oil

2 T butter

1 lb turkey cutlets

1 T capers

2 lemons

Flour

Directions
Dredge cutlets in flour while melting butter in oil over medium heat. Add cutlets to pan and sauté until done (about 3 minutes on each side). Remove cutlets. Stir juice of two lemons and capers into pan over medium high heat and scrape to loosen brown bits from pan. Add cutlets back into pan and turn. When sauce begins to thicken, remove and serve.

Preparation Time: 10 minutes

Side by Side
Noodles tossed with olive oil and garlic powder are a nice side with this dish. Rice also works well. Serve with steamed vegetable of your choice.

Turkey Parmigiana

Ingredients

4 turkey cutlets

1/2 c bread crumbs seasoned with 1/2 t Italian seasoning

1 egg, beaten with fork

4 T butter or margarine (1/2 stick)

1 c favorite marinara sauce

1 c grated mozzarella cheese

Parmesan cheese, grated

Directions

Preheat oven to 400°. Melt butter. Dip cutlets in egg and bread crumbs. Sauté in butter for 2 to 2 1/2 minutes on each side over medium high heat. Put cutlets in greased baking dish (use non-stick cooking spray). Sprinkle each cutlet with 1 teaspoon Parmesan cheese. Spoon marinara sauce over cutlets and top with mozzarella. Bake uncovered until cheese is melted (about 5 minutes).

Preparation Time: 15 minutes working time/5 minutes baking time

Side by Side

Serve with noodles tossed lightly with olive oil, garlic powder and chopped tomatoes or a light marinara sauce. A green salad with an Italian or vinaigrette dressing is a winner. Try the mustard vinaigrette (page 110).

Turkey Cutlets with Lemon and Parsley

Ingredients

4 turkey cutlets

1/2 c bread crumbs

1/2 teaspoon Italian or pasta seasoning blend

1 egg, beaten with fork

4 T butter or margarine (1/2 stick)

2 T fresh parsley, minced

Juice of one lemon

Directions

Mix bread crumbs and Italian seasoning. Melt butter in skillet. Dip cutlets in egg and then bread crumbs. Sauté in butter over medium high heat for 2 to 2 1/2 minutes on each side. Remove cutlets. Squeeze lemon juice into butter and add parsley. Stir. Put cutlets in pan over medium low heat and turn in lemon-parsley mixture until coated. Remove and serve immediately.

Preparation Time: 10 minutes

*	To save time, skip the bread crumbs and merely dredge the cutlets in flour and then follow the recipe. Or, use pre-seasoned bread crumbs.

*	If you season your own bread crumbs and do not have Italian seasoning, substitute 1/2 teaspoon crushed oregano, thyme, marjoram, or parsley flakes.

*	Another quick lemony dish you might like to try is made this way: Brown 1 pound boneless chicken thighs, breasts or tenders. Add 1 8-ounce bottle Italian salad dressing. To speed cooking, cut up the meat as it cooks. Add 3 tablespoons instant lemonade crystals. This can be adjusted to taste. If you like your sauce a little sweeter, add a teaspoon of sugar. Sprinkle generously with fresh cracked black pepper and serve chicken over white rice.

Side by Side

This dish goes nicely with buttered noodles or white rice and a spinach or green salad. Since this is a light dish, you can serve it with a creamy salad dressing like Parmesan (page 109) or 999 Island (page 108).

Chicken with Orange Sauce

Ingredients
4 boneless chicken breasts or thighs

1 T vegetable oil

1 onion, chopped

3/4 c orange marmalade

1/4 c white wine or orange juice

Juice of 1/2 lemon (optional)

Directions
Brown onion in oil. When translucent, add chicken and, if necessary to keep skillet from drying out, add up to 1/4 cup wine or orange juice (or water). Lower heat and brown meat on both sides. To speed cooking, cut meat into smaller pieces as it cooks and keep it covered when you are not working with meat. Mix marmalade with a fork to break it up and pour over meat. Cook over medium high heat for an additional 2 or 3 minutes or until meat is cooked through. Squeeze with fresh lemon if you like a tangier sauce.

Preparation Time: 10-15 minutes, depending upon size of boneless chicken pieces used

*   A tangy orange sauce variation of this recipe can be made in the following way: Sauté a large chopped onion in a skillet over high heat. Keep it moving to avoid burning it. When onion is soft, add one cup orange juice, 1/2 cup balsamic vinegar or red wine vinegar, and sugar to taste (about 3 to 4 tablespoons if using balsamic vinegar and about 1/4 cup to 1/3 cup if using red wine vinegar). Add chicken tenders or other boneless chicken pieces and poach in juice until chicken is done. When adjusting sugar to your taste, always start with less and add more if you want a sweeter sauce. If you use balsamic vinegar, you will probably use less sugar to get the right taste balance than if you use any other vinegar.

Side by Side
Serve this dish with buttered noodles or white or brown rice. Couscous also accompanies it well. Couscous and carrots (page 123) is a tasty vegetable side dish. Try greens dressed with balsamic vinaigrette (page 107).

Chicken with Honey Mustard Sauce

Ingredients

1 lb chicken tenders or boneless thighs

1 T vegetable oil

3/8 c honey

1/4 c Dijon mustard

1 T apple cider vinegar

3 T water or white wine

1 t garlic powder

1/4 t ground black pepper

Flour

Directions

Dredge chicken pieces in flour and brown in oil in covered skillet over medium high heat. While chicken browns, mix remaining ingredients in a bowl and whisk. Turn chicken, pour sauce over meat, cover and simmer until meat is done.

Preparation Time: 10 minutes

Side by Side

Serve this dish over couscous or rice. Steamed vegetables provide a good accompaniment with a green salad tossed with a light vinaigrette dressing.

Creamy Chicken

Ingredients

4 boneless, skinless chicken breasts or thighs

2 T butter or margarine

1/2 c milk

2 T Dijon mustard

1/4 c pickles—gherkins or cornishons, chopped

Salt and pepper

Flour

Directions

Dredge chicken pieces in flour. Brown in butter over medium heat. Add milk and turn heat to medium low. Salt and pepper lightly. Cover and cook down for about five minutes. Check occasionally. If sauce begins to get too thick, add a little water. Add mustard and gherkins (or cornishons) and stir until sauce is fully blended.

Preparation Time: 15 minutes

* Preparation time can be shortened by using 8 boneless chicken tenders instead of larger pieces of meat. The sauce cooks very quickly so the length of cooking time is dependent upon the size of meat pieces.

* You can omit the gherkins and/or cornishons entirely, if you prefer.

* This mild sauce also works well over flaky white fish such as sea bass.

Side by Side

Greens dressed with a sweet and tangy salad dressing (page 106) or mustard vinaigrette (page 110) go well with this dish. Salad with Italian or Caesar dressing is also good. A mild vegetable such as carrots or green beans is a good choice as a side.

Italian Chicken

Ingredients

4 boneless chicken breasts or thighs

1 14-oz jar marinara or spaghetti sauce

6 fresh basil leaves, chopped

1/2 c grated Parmesan cheese

1/2 c grated mozzarella cheese

Directions

Cook chicken in covered skillet over medium heat. If the pan is too dry, add a little water so that it does not burn. As the chicken cooks, mix remaining ingredients in a bowl. When chicken is done cooking (about 5 minutes), pour sauce over it, reduce heat to low, cover, and simmer for 5 to 10 minutes (until cheese is melted). Serve over pasta if you choose or as a main dish with salad and vegetable.

Preparation Time: 10 to 15 minutes

*   Without adding much cooking time, you can sauté the chicken with a chopped onion and minced garlic clove. Then, follow the remaining directions.

*   An alternate way to make this dish is to bake it in the oven. It is even better this way as the sauce blends with the cheese and chicken juices while baking. To make baked Italian chicken, put chicken in a baking pan, cover with marinara sauce, top with lots of mozzarella cheese and bake covered for 45 minutes to an hour (until chicken is done) at 350°. The working time then is less than five minutes although the dish is not ready to serve for about an hour.

Side by Side

Serve over spaghetti or capellini noodles or with polenta on the side. Broccoli is a good side dish choice. Serve greens with Italian or Caesar dressing or try the roasted red pepper and Gorgonzola salad (page 112).

Chicken Ponzu

Ingredients

4 pieces boneless chicken

1 T vegetable oil

1 onion, chopped

1 clove garlic, minced

1/2 c sliced mushrooms

1 c broccoli flowerlets

1 red bell pepper, sliced or chopped

1/3 c soy sauce

Juice of 3 limes

Pinch of sugar

Directions

Brown garlic and onion in oil. Add chicken and brown on one side (3-4 minutes). Turn chicken over to finish cooking and add vegetables. Cover pan and let cook over medium low heat for 2 to 3 minutes. Mix soy, lime juice and sugar to make the ponzu sauce. Pour half or all of sauce over chicken and vegetables and cook for another minute or so. Serve with white rice.

Preparation Time: less than 15 minutes

* If you don't want to chop garlic, use a teaspoon of minced garlic from a jar or 1/2 teaspoon of garlic powder. If you use garlic powder, sprinkle it over the meat when you add it.

Side by Side

Serve with white rice or pair with the warm rice salad with shrimp (page 118). You can use any mild vegetables you choose with this dish. A stir-fried vegetable such as celery or snow peas works well.

Pork Medallions with Chutney Sauce

Ingredients

1 lb pork tenderloin, cut into medallions

1 onion, chopped

1 T vegetable oil

1/2 c white wine

1 8-oz jar Major Grey's chutney

Directions

Sauté onion in oil for about 1 minute. Add medallions and brown on each side over medium high heat. Add wine, cover and cook for about 6 minutes or until pork is cooked through. Add chutney and stir.

Preparation Time: less than 10 minutes

*   Serve with curry style accompaniments such as sliced bananas, coconut, peanuts and rice.

Side by Side

In addition to the curry style accompaniments described above, this dish goes well with peas or carrots as a side dish. Rice would be the starch of choice. Consider pairing this dish with greens and mustard vinaigrette (page 110).

Pork Chops with Apricot Mustard Sauce

Ingredients
6 thin cut pork chops (a little over 1 lb)

1/2 c apricot preserves

2 T Dijon mustard

1 t minced chives

Vegetable oil

Directions
Mix preserves, mustard, and chives. Put 1 tablespoon oil in skillet over high heat. Brown chops quickly on each side. Once turned, lower heat and spread chops with half of sauce mixture. Turn again and spread with remaining sauce. Cover and simmer for 3 to 4 minutes over medium low heat. Serves 4. Light eaters take one chop. Bigger appetites need two.

Preparation Time: 10 to 15 minutes

Side by Side
Serve with carrots, peas or corn as a side dish. Serve over white rice, buttered noodles or couscous. Greens with a balsamic vinaigrette (page 107) or honey mustard dressing would accompany well.

Pork Medallions with Cherries and Onions

Ingredients

1 lb pork tenderloin, cut into medallions

8 oz dried bing cherries

1/2 c sugar

2/3 c water

1/2 c red wine vinegar

1 onion, chopped

1 T vegetable oil

1/2 t ground ginger

Dash cinnamon

Cornstarch

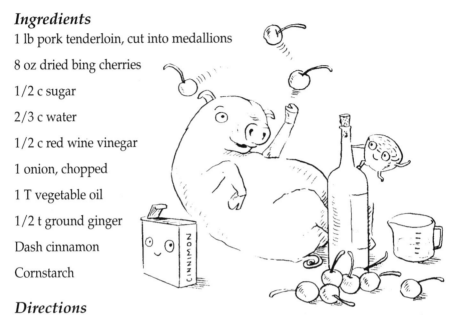

Directions

Cut pork tenderloin into medallions about 1/4 to 1/2-inch thick. Dredge in cornstarch. Sauté onion in oil over high heat for about 1 minute. Add medallions, sear and flip over. Add cherries, sugar, water, vinegar, ginger and cinnamon. Turn heat down to medium high and cook covered for about 2 to 3 minutes. Remove medallions to a side dish. Turn heat onto high and cook sauce for 5 minutes. If necessary, thicken with additional cornstarch. To do this, mix a teaspoon cornstarch with some of the sauce and then drizzle into the pan and stir quickly. Remove from heat and drizzle sauce over pork medallions.

Preparation Time: 15 minutes

* You can dredge medallions in flour rather than cornstarch, if you prefer.

Side by Side

This dish goes well with white rice or couscous. Tasty side dishes are peas, green beans, cauliflower or carrots. Greens with sweet and tangy dressing (page 106), balsamic vinaigrette (page 107), or honey mustard dressing complement this dish well.

Shepherd's Pie

Ingredients

1 lb ground turkey or lean beef

1 onion, chopped

1 c frozen mixed peas and carrots

1/2 t each crushed thyme and parsley

1 can cream of mushroom soup

3 cups mashed potatoes

Dash garlic powder (optional)

Directions

Put water on to make 3 cups instant mashed potatoes. As you sauté meat, onion, peas and carrots with spices, prepare potatoes according to package directions, adding garlic powder if you choose. When meat is done, add mushroom soup and stir to blend. Put into 9-inch pie or cake plate and cover with mashed potatoes. Serve immediately or you can keep it warm in a 200° oven until you are ready to eat. Alternatively, dot mashed potatoes with butter or sprinkle with grated Parmesan cheese and put the pie under the broiler for 3 to 5 minutes until the potatoes brown slightly in spots.

Preparation Time: 15 minutes (20 minutes if you broil the pie)

* If you want to spice up your potatoes a bit, add 1/4 to 1/3 cup light sour cream to them. Alternately, you can add a little grated Parmesan or cheddar cheese.

* To make it pretty for serving, dust mashed potatoes with paprika, fresh ground pepper or parsley flakes.

* You can reverse the structure of this pie. Put the mashed potatoes in the pan first and then add the meat filling. Then there's no need to broil it at all.

Side by Side

Serve this hearty dish with a salad of mixed greens and a light dressing or with broccoli (page 119) or green pea (page 117) salad. It also goes well with steamed vegetables such as cauliflower, broccoli and green beans on the side.

Beef Stroganoff

Ingredients

2 T vegetable oil

1 onion, chopped

1 c mushrooms, sliced

1/2 lb steak (beef stroganoff strips, stir-fry strips, or New York steak cut into small pieces)

1 10.5-oz can cream of mushroom soup

1 T catsup

1/2-3/4 c sour cream

Directions

Brown onion, meat and mushrooms in oil over medium high heat. Turn heat down to medium. Add mushroom soup and catsup and stir until smooth. Mix sour cream with a 1/2 cup sauce from pan and then add sour cream to mixture. Serve over noodles or rice.

Preparation Time: less than 15 minutes

*   If you don't have cream of mushroom soup, dredge meat in flour and brown it with onions and mushroom. Add a little water to the skillet. Lower heat, sprinkle with salt and garlic powder, and simmer in covered pan. When meat is done, mix sauce from the pan into sour cream to thin it. Then add thinned sour cream to pan. Stir and serve.

Side by Side

Serve over mashed potatoes or noodles. Good side dish vegetables are corn, broccoli, or cauliflower. Try the broccoli salad (page 119) as an accompaniment or greens dressed with balsamic vinaigrette (page 107).

Sloppy BBQ Burgers

Ingredients
1 lb lean ground beef or turkey

1 onion, chopped

1/2 bell pepper, chopped (optional)

1/2-3/4 c barbeque sauce

4 hamburger buns

Directions
Brown beef with onion and bell pepper until meat is no longer pink. Add barbeque sauce and stir. Serve on hamburger buns.

Preparation Time: less than 10 minutes

* You can add 1/2 teaspoon garlic powder to the meat as you brown it to add to the flavor.

* If you do not have barbeque sauce, an easy make-at-home version is 1/2 cup catsup, 1 tablespoon Dijon mustard, 1 tablespoon red wine vinegar and 1 tablespoon soy sauce. For a sweeter sauce, add 1 tablespoon honey.

Side by Side
Serve with sliced fresh fruit or a fruit salad and pasta salad with feta cheese (page 116). If you choose to serve a green salad, any dressing of your choice will work fine, but consider Parmesan dressing (page 109) or 999 Island dressing (page 108). Picnic-style sides such as coleslaw, potato or macaroni salad and baked beans are fun touches as well.

Sweet Pepper Salmon Steaks

Ingredients

1 lb salmon steaks or fillets

1 small onion, chopped

1/2 red bell pepper, chopped

3 T balsamic vinegar

3 T butter

Directions

Sauté chopped onion and bell pepper in butter over medium high heat. Stir in balsamic vinegar. Lower heat to medium low and add salmon. Cook covered for 3 to 4 minutes on each side.

Preparation Time: 10 minutes

Side by Side

This fish dish goes well with white rice or couscous. Steamed asparagus, broccoli, or squash are nice accompaniments. For a salad, try romaine with oranges and avocados (page 111) or roasted red pepper and Gorgonzola salad (page 112).

Sea Bass with Onions and Oranges

Ingredients

1 T vegetable oil

1 1/2 lb sea bass fillets, cut into 2 by 4-inch pieces

1 onion, sliced

1 orange, sliced

1/2 c red seedless grapes, cut in half

1/2 c orange juice

1 T butter or margarine

Dash nutmeg

Directions

Put oil in large skillet over medium heat. Put in a layer of onion slices, then a layer of orange slices. Add sea bass fillets. Drizzle with orange juice and dot top with butter. Sprinkle lightly with nutmeg and add grapes. Cover and increase heat to medium high. Fish steams on its bed in about 10 to 12 minutes. Baste occasionally with sauce from pan.

Preparation Time: 15 minutes

*   This recipe works well with any mild, white fish.

Side by Side

Couscous is a particularly nice complement to this dish, but it can also be served over a bed of linguine or other thick noodles. A lightly flavored vegetable such as green beans or carrots goes well.

White Fish on a Bed

Ingredients

1 lb boneless fish fillets (orange roughy, sea bass, halibut)

1 onion, sliced thin

1 c sun-dried tomatoes

8 large fresh basil leaves, cut into 1/4 inch strips

1 T vegetable oil

1 large lemon

Directions

Put tomatoes into hot water to soak while you cut up onion and basil. Put oil in skillet and heat over medium high heat. Lay onion slices on the bottom of the pan. Put soaked tomatoes around on bed of onion and top with basil leaf strips. Lay fish on this vegetable bed and drizzle with the juice of one large lemon. Reduce heat to medium low. Cover and cook fish for about 5 to 7 minutes. Turn fish in the middle of cooking. If you need to add liquid as fish cooks, add a tablespoon or two of the water in which the tomatoes soaked.

Preparation Time: 15 minutes

Side by Side

Serve with white or brown rice. A sweet dressing, either vinaigrette-style or creamy, on a green salad offers a nice complement to this dish. Almond asparagus (page 125) and broccoli are good vegetable choices.

Salmon with Paprika Sauce

Ingredients
4 salmon fillets

4 T butter or margarine, melted

2 t Worcestershire sauce

2 T chives, chopped

1/4 t paprika

Directions
Put 1 tablespoon butter in skillet and brown salmon over medium low heat. Cover and cook for 4 to 5 minutes on each side. Melt remaining butter in microwave and mix with Worcestershire sauce, chives and paprika. Pour sauce over salmon when you turn it.

Preparation Time: less than 15 minutes

Side by Side
This dish is great with any number of vegetables from steamed broccoli, asparagus or green beans to sautéed sweet bell pepper and onions. Serve with white rice.

Halibut Steaks with Tangy Soy and Onions

Ingredients
1 T vegetable oil

1 onion, chopped

1 t minced garlic or two minced cloves

1/4 t ginger powder (optional)

1 lb halibut steaks, cut into 1 by 3-inch pieces

1/4 c soy sauce

1/4 c red wine vinegar

2 T sugar

Directions
Sauté onion, garlic, and ginger in oil over medium high heat until onions are translucent. Add halibut steaks and soy sauce mixture. Cover and cook for about 4 minutes on each side or until meat is white and flaky.

Preparation Time: 15 minutes

*   If you have fresh ginger, a few medallions minced offer a much more lively taste than ginger powder, although mincing them adds a few minutes to the preparation time.

*   The sauce can be made in the measuring cup or you can pour the ingredients directly into the pan and stir them into the onions.

*   If you prefer a less tangy sauce, adjust the vinegar by using 2 or 3 tablespoons vinegar and 3 or 2 tablespoons water, respectively, to make 1/4 cup.

Side by Side
Try this dish with rice and steamed broccoli or stir-fried bok choy or celery on the side. To stir fry such vegetables, cut them into 1/2 to 1 inch pieces, put them in a pan with a tablespoon hot vegetable oil, and stir them quickly and constantly until they turn bright green—about 2 minutes. Season with a splash of soy or dash of salt and garlic powder.

Tuna and Stuff

Ingredients
1 T vegetable oil

1/2 onion, chopped

1 c broccoli flowerets, diced

1/2 c mushrooms, sliced

1 stalk celery, diced

1 12-oz can tuna, drained

1 10-3/4-oz can cream of mushroom soup

1/4 c water

Minute-style rice

Directions
Cook rice according to package directions while you make the tuna part of the recipe. Brown onion in oil. Add remaining vegetables when onions are soft. Stir fry vegetables over medium high heat until they turn bright green. Add tuna, soup and water. Stir to heat and blend ingredients. Serve over hot rice.

Preparation Time: 5 minutes

*   You can substitute any vegetables. Good choices are green peas, green beans, zucchini, bell pepper, and water chestnuts.

*   Here's another quick tuna favorite: Mix 1/2 small diced onion, 1 cup frozen peas (thawed), 1/2 7.5-ounce bag crushed potato chips, 2 12-ounce cans drained tuna, 1 can cream of mushroom soup, and 1 8-ounce can water chestnuts (drained, sliced and chopped). Put into baking dish, top with remaining chips, and heat for 20 minutes at 400°.

*   For another very fast tuna casserole that is a big hit with kids, see the "Cook As You Are" section of this book under "Lotsa Pasta" (page 17).

Side by Side
Serve with a green salad and sliced fruit. Or, try it with broccoli (page 119) or green pea (page 117) salad.

Tossed Tuna Salad

Ingredients
1 heart of romaine, chopped

1 12-oz can tuna, drained

1 15-oz can cannellini or white beans, drained and rinsed

1 tomato, chopped

2-3 T chopped red onion (or 1 chopped green onion)

Sweet and tangy dressing (page 106)

Directions
Drain beans and tuna. Place in bowl with chopped lettuce, tomato and onion. Toss with dressing and serve.

Preparation Time: less than 10 minutes

* This is a hearty dinner salad idea that can be modified as you choose based on ingredients you have available. Black beans work well and added vegetables such as diced bell pepper, cucumber and carrots are good. While a light vinaigrette-style dressing is suggested, this salad is also tasty with ranch or other heavier dressings. You might also want to add a handful of grated cheddar cheese.

Side by Side
Serve this salad with crusty bread with basil butter (page 44) or onion focaccia (page 43).

Teriyaki Whatever

Ingredients

1 lb boneless fish or meat pieces (salmon steaks, tuna, white fish, chicken, beef or pork)

1 onion, chopped

1/2 c soy sauce

1/2 c sugar

1/2 t garlic powder

1-2 T vegetable oil

Directions

Sauté onion in oil until translucent. Mix sugar, soy sauce and garlic powder in a separate bowl. Place meat in skillet and cover with teriyaki sauce. Cover and cook over medium low heat for about 3 to 5 minutes on each side depending upon the kind of meat. Turn once. Check occasionally to make sure pan is not drying out. If it is, add a little water. Serve with rice.

Preparation Time: 10-15 minutes

*   You can adjust the teriyaki sauce to your taste. If you like it saltier, add a little more soy. If you like it sweeter, add a little more sugar.

*   You can make the teriyaki with or without the garlic powder. Also, if you want to get fancy, delete the garlic powder from the sauce and sauté one or two minced garlic cloves with the onion. Heat it up with a splash of red pepper flakes.

*   If you want to add a vegetable to this dish, you can steam broccoli flowerlets in the microwave for a couple of minutes. Drain them and throw them into the skillet after you remove the meat to serve it. Stir the broccoli to coat and pour sauce with broccoli over the meat to serve.

Side by Side

Serve this dish over or with white rice or try it with warm rice salad with shrimp (page 118). Steamed broccoli is also great on the side. Steamed carrots and celery are also good side dishes. Greens tossed with French dressing or a vinaigrette also work well.

Ratatouille with Eggs

Ingredients

1 clove garlic, minced

1 onion, chopped

1 T olive oil

1 large zucchini, sliced into quarter-inch thick medallions

2 tomatoes, chopped

2 Japanese eggplants, peeled and chopped

1/2 t salt

1/2 t thyme

Pepper to taste

4 eggs

Directions

Put the oil in skillet and mince garlic and chop onion into the pan as the oil warms over medium heat. Stir occasionally as you slice zucchini, tomatoes and eggplant into skillet. Sauté. Add salt, thyme and pepper and stir again. Add 1/3 cup water and cover to simmer for several minutes over low heat. When the zucchini is soft, break four eggs over the ratatouille in the pan and cover for about 2 minutes to cook eggs. Serve with rice, noodles or garlic toast.

Preparation Time: 15 minutes

*   What makes this meal so easy is that, once you start the garlic and onion cooking, you merely chop the remaining vegetables directly into the pan and stir as you go. Also, it can be made with just about any fresh vegetables you have on hand. The tomatoes and zucchini are important, but you can use bell pepper, chopped broccoli heads, or green beans. You can also add a half cup firm tofu sliced into julienne-style strips when you add the zucchini.

Side by Side

Without the eggs, this dish makes a nice pasta sauce. You can also serve the ratatouille over scrambled eggs, but this makes it a two-pan dinner to clean up. You might want to serve it with a green salad or sliced fruit.

Potato Sauté with Tofu and Cheese

Ingredients

2 T vegetable oil

1 large onion, chopped

2 c sliced mushrooms

1 lb frozen cubed hash brown potatoes

1/2 t each parsley and thyme flakes

1/2 lb tofu, cubed (medium firmness)

2 c cheddar cheese, grated

Salt and pepper to taste

Directions

Brown onion in oil over high heat for 1 minute. Add mushrooms, potatoes, parsley, and thyme. Turn heat down to medium, cover and let cook for about 5 to 7 minutes. Stir occasionally. If pan begins to dry out, add 1/4 cup water and cover. Salt and pepper to taste. Stir tofu into potatoes; cover and cook for 1 minute. Add grated cheese. Stir into mixture slightly. Turn off heat and cover to let cheese melt.

Preparation Time: 15-20 minutes

* Garnish with sliced tomatoes and/or sliced avocados.

* You can add frozen peas or corn. If you choose to add vegetables, add them with potatoes.

Side by Side

This dish is good with dark green vegetables on the side. Try sautéed broccoli, spinach or green beans. Asparagus, zucchini and celery are also good on the side. For salad, try greens with mustard vinaigrette (page 110).

Polenta with Three-Mushroom Sauce

Ingredients
1 T olive oil

1 small onion, chopped

2 c white mushrooms, sliced

1 c crimini mushrooms, sliced

1 c portabella mushrooms, chopped

1 T garlic powder

1 T sugar

1/4 c balsamic vinegar

Polenta (Buy it readymade in the refrigerated section of the market, or make your own with the recipe below.)

Directions
Sauté onion in olive oil about one minute (until onions are beginning to soften). Add remaining ingredients (except polenta) and a little water. Turn heat to medium low and cover. Cook for about three minutes, stirring once or twice. Keep covered when not stirring. Serve over polenta heated according to package directions or use recipe below.

Preparation Time: 10 minutes

* Ingredients for a quick polenta are 1 cup cornmeal, 1 cup corn, 1 small chopped onion, 1/2 t salt, and 3 cups water. Sauté onion with 1 T olive oil in sauce pan. Add remaining ingredients and bring to a boil, stirring frequently. When corn mixture is thick, spoon into bowls or onto plates and cover with mushroom sauce. You can add 1 cup peas, 1/4 to 1/3 cup grated Parmesan cheese, 2 T fresh diced basil or sautéed garlic cloves or sweet red pepper strips to this polenta for a change of pace.

Side by Side
Almost any vegetable serves well on the side. Options include zucchini, green beans, snow peas, and carrots. Try a green salad dressed with a light or creamy dressing. Green pea salad (page 117) works well with this dish too.

Pasta with Artichoke Sauce

Ingredients

1 14-oz can artichoke bottoms in water

1/4 c grated Parmesan cheese

1 t sun-dried tomato bits

1 t fresh rosemary, minced

1/2 t crushed garlic or 1 minced garlic clove

1/4 t fresh cracked black pepper

Pasta such as fusilli (corkscrew) or penne

Directions

Put on pasta to cook. Drain and reserve liquid from artichokes. Mash artichokes with potato masher until only small chunks remain. Mince a sprig of fresh rosemary. Combine all ingredients and add reserved liquid one tablespoon at a time until sauce is the consistency you like—probably 4 to 7 tablespoons. Drain cooked pasta and rinse briefly with hot water. Toss with sauce and serve with extra Parmesan cheese.

Preparation Time: 10-20 minutes, depending on the type of pasta used

*   A sturdy pasta is important to the success of this dish. Try penne, pennette, cut ziti, fusilli or bow tie pasta.

*   If you prefer a finer artichoke paste, put artichoke bottoms into a blender or food processor to puree, but doing it by hand works just fine and requires less clean up.

*   Leftover artichoke pasta can be refrigerated and turned into a good pasta salad. Add diced green onion and 1 chopped tomato or other vegetable of your choice such as bell pepper. Drizzle with olive oil and toss all ingredients. Sprinkle with a little Parmesan cheese to serve.

Side by Side

This is a tart dish that goes nicely with a mild vegetable such as peas, zucchini, sweet red pepper or carrots. A good salad dressing is one with a sweet edge such as sweet and tangy (page 106), balsamic vinaigrette (page 107) or even 999 Island (page 108).

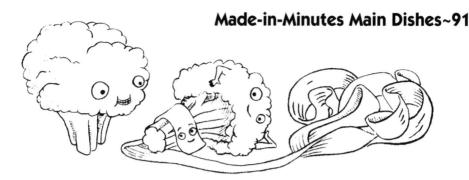

Linguine with Gorgonzola and Broccoli Sauce

Ingredients

1/2 c milk

1/2 c Gorgonzola cheese, crumbled

1 c broccoli flowerets, diced

Linguine

Directions

Put pasta on to cook. Dice broccoli and steam in a covered container with 1 teaspoon water in the microwave on high for 1-1/2 minutes. Remove and set aside. Put milk and cheese in bowl and microwave for 1-1/2 to 2 minutes on high heat. Slightly mash cheese into warm milk. Add broccoli and serve over drained noodles.

Preparation Time: less than 10 minutes

* This dish can be made with regular or with skim milk. The sauce is thin, but since it is rich it works well with the large noodles and is not overpowering. Many picky eaters can enjoy this dish even though made with a mild blue cheese.

* This dish can also be made even more quickly without the broccoli and served as either a side or main dish with a salad.

* Garnish with cracked pepper if your diners choose.

Side by Side

Serve with a green salad tossed with an Italian, vinaigrette, sweet and tangy (page 106) or balsamic vinaigrette (page 107) dressing. Keep the dressing light. Fresh fruit is also good with this dish.

Carbonara

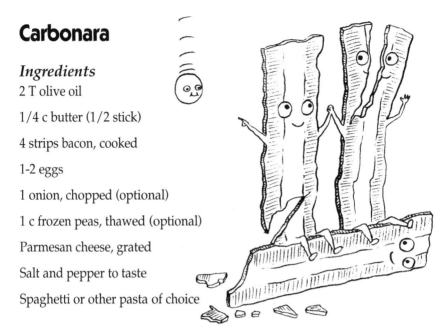

Ingredients

2 T olive oil

1/4 c butter (1/2 stick)

4 strips bacon, cooked

1-2 eggs

1 onion, chopped (optional)

1 c frozen peas, thawed (optional)

Parmesan cheese, grated

Salt and pepper to taste

Spaghetti or other pasta of choice

Directions

Put water on to cook spaghetti. Brown bacon until crisp. Remove from pan and pour off excess grease. Crumble when cool to touch. Melt butter with olive oil. If you use onions, brown them now. Add peas and bacon when onions are translucent. Drain spaghetti and put into skillet. Toss over medium heat to coat spaghetti with oil. Make a hole in center of skillet and drop in one or two eggs. Scramble them into spaghetti until hard. Sprinkle with Parmesan cheese and salt and pepper to taste.

Preparation Time: 10-15 minutes, depending on the kind of meat you use

*   This dish can be made with bacon, diced ham, diced proscuitto, or even chopped lunch meat. This dish can also be made without the onions or peas. Another way to cook the egg is to break it into the pan with the vegetables, put the steaming hot pasta into the pan, and toss. The hot pasta cooks the egg.

*   This dish is a perennial favorite in our house. It's the kind of dish you can make when you have nothing in the house. It is a perfect last minute meal.

Side by Side

This dish is good with a mixed green salad dressed with an oil and vinegar type dressing. Broccoli is a good side dish.

Capellini alla Checca

Ingredients
2 T olive oil

2-3 cloves garlic, minced

6-8 leaves fresh basil, rolled and cut into 1/4 inch strips

2 tomatoes, chopped

2 T sundried tomato pieces

Parmesan cheese

Capellini

Directions
Put water on to cook pasta. As you cook the pasta, put olive oil into skillet with garlic. Brown the garlic over medium high heat. Lower heat to medium and add tomatoes, basil and sun-dried tomato pieces. When pasta is done, drain it, rinse in hot water, and pour into skillet. Toss with sautéed tomatoes and seasonings. Put onto plates and sprinkle with Parmesan cheese.

Preparation Time: 10 minutes

*   Capellini is a favorite pasta with this light and easy sauce. It cooks quickly as it is done in about 3 minutes. You can also use spaghetti and spaghettini with this dish. Thicker pastas are a matter of personal taste.

*   If you like garlic, use more garlic with this recipe as garlic is what makes many diners go back for more. Also, you can sauté a chopped onion with the garlic and add this to the dish, if you choose.

*   You might prefer to toss the pasta and tomatoes with the cheese so that the cheese is dispersed through the hot pasta.

*   Alternate cheeses to try with this pasta dish are crumbled feta, chunks of Brie melted into the hot pasta as you toss it with the sautéed vegetables, and grated mozzarella which also needs to be tossed with the hot pasta.

Side by Side
Serve with a lightly dressed green salad. Italian and Caesar dressings work well or try the roasted red pepper and Gorgonzola salad (page 112).

Spaghetti with Hearty Meat Sauce

Ingredients

1/2 lb ground beef or turkey

1 onion, chopped

1 t Italian seasoning

1/2 t garlic powder

1 26-oz jar marinara sauce (your favorite)

Parmesan cheese

Spaghetti or other pasta

Directions

Brown ground meat with onion and seasonings. Add marinara sauce. Stir to warm. Serve over hot pasta and garnish with grated Parmesan cheese.

Preparation Time: 10 minutes

*   If the sauce seems too bland when you are done, add a little more Italian seasoning, crushed oregano, parsley or whatever Italian spices you like best. Jazz up this sauce anyway you like by adding sliced mushrooms, small-cut broccoli heads or zucchini as you brown the meat. You can also splash in a little red or white wine after you add the sauce.

*   If you don't have ground meat in the house, a traditional Italian pasta sauce uses canned tuna. Simply brown onion and add a 12-ounce can of tuna (drained) when you add the marinara sauce and seasonings and you have a new version of an old favorite. Sometimes sliced black olives are added to the sauce with the tuna. Or, turn this recipe into a vegetarian dish by eliminating the meat and beginning with sautéed vegetables only.

Side by Side

Sautéed zucchini or broccoli are good side dishes for this hearty main dish. Serve with a salad tossed with a vinaigrette-style dressing.

Veggie Lasagna with White Sauce

Ingredients

2 cans cream of mushroom soup

2/3 can water

2/3 c mayonnaise

2 c each frozen peas and carrots, thawed

1 c mushrooms, sliced

1 onion, chopped

2 t garlic powder

1 pkg chopped spinach, thawed

3 c cheddar cheese, grated

3 c jack cheese, grated

Lasagna pasta, uncooked

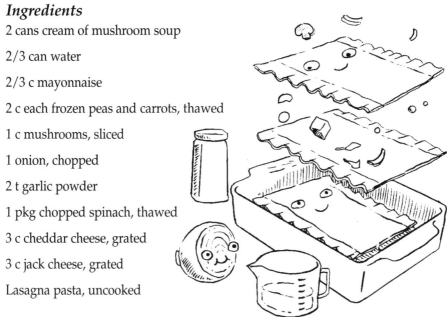

Directions

Mix first 7 ingredients in a large bowl to make sauce. Preheat oven to 425°. Spray 9 by 13 inch pan with non-stick cooking spray. Layer ingredients as follows: Spread a little sauce on bottom. Cover with 2 to 3 pieces of uncooked lasagna. Then spread a little more sauce, 1/2 the spinach, 1/2 the cheese. Repeat this layering ending with pasta, sauce, then cheese. Cover tightly with foil. Bake at 425° for 15 minutes; then reduce heat to 375° for another 45 minutes.

Preparation Time: 15-20 minutes working time/1 hour baking time

Side by Side

Steamed carrots, zucchini, or sautéed mixed sweet peppers are a nice side to this casserole-style dish. Serve also with a salad dressed in a vinaigrette-style dressing.

Shrimp Pasta with Tomatoes and Herbed Feta

Ingredients

1/2 lb salad shrimp, cooked and thawed

1 onion, chopped

1 clove garlic, minced

2 tomatoes, chopped

2 T olive oil

1 t Italian seasoning

2 oz herbed feta cheese, crumbled

Pasta

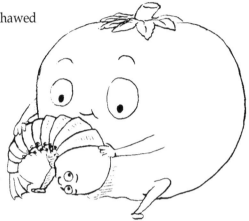

Directions

If your shrimp is not thawed, put it in a colander and run cold water over it. As the shrimp is thawing, put on a pasta of your choice to cook. Next, sauté onion and garlic in oil. Add tomatoes and shrimp when onion becomes translucent. Sauté for a minute or so to warm and soften tomatoes. Set aside if pasta is not yet cooked. When pasta is cooked, put it into the sauté pan, add seasoning and cheese, and toss all ingredients.

Preparation Time: 10 minutes

*   You can make this dish with a leftover cooked, diced chicken breast if you don't want to use shrimp. To quick-cook raw chicken for this dish, steam a boneless breast or several chicken tenders in the microwave with a little water in a covered dish on high for 2 minutes. Rinse with cold water and then dice the chicken into the pan. The chicken is done when the pinkness is gone.

Side by Side

Suggested side dish vegetables are asparagus, zucchini, and sweet red pepper with onion and garlic. Mixed greens dressed with a sweet and tangy dressing (page 106) or balsamic vinaigrette (page 107) blend well with this tangy dish.

Black Bean and Corn Tacorito

Ingredients
1 15-oz can black beans, drained

1 15-oz can kernel corn, drained

1 onion, chopped

1/2 t garlic powder

1/4 c diced fresh cilantro

Grated jack cheese

Soft taco-size flour tortillas

Directions
Brown the onion over medium high heat until translucent. Add beans and garlic. Mash beans slightly into onions and mix well. In a separate pan, warm up corn. To make four tacoritos, spread each tortilla with bean mixture, sprinkle with jack cheese, and top with corn and fresh cilantro. Fold in sides of tortilla and roll.

Preparation Time: 10 minutes

Side by Side
Serve this dish with avocado and onions salad (page 113) or greens dressed with avocado dressing (page 107).

Mexican Lasagna

Ingredients

Flour tortillas

1 16-oz jar mild tomato salsa

1/2 lb ground beef or turkey

1 onion, chopped

1 c lettuce, shredded

1 tomato, chopped

2 c cheddar cheese, grated

Directions

Preheat oven to 450°. Brown ground meat with onion. While the meat is cooking, chop tomato and shred lettuce. Put 2 tablespoons salsa on bottom of 9 by 13 inch baking dish. Cover bottom of dish with a layer of flour tortillas. On this base, layer meat, tomato, lettuce, cheese (reserving 1/2 cup), and salsa (reserving 1/2 cup). Cover with another layer of tortillas over which you spread remaining salsa and cheese. Cover and bake for 20 minutes or until cheese melts.

Preparation Time: 10-15 minutes working time/20 minutes baking time

*   This recipe serves 4 to 6. Double the ingredients and make a lasagna two full layers thick to serve 8 to 12. This requires you to increase the baking time to 30 to 40 minutes, but you can use the dish easily to cover two meals. Leftover casserole can also be frozen for later use.

*   Substitute refried beans for the meat to make this dish vegetarian. Or add refried beans to the meat dish. Make sure you spread the beans on the tortillas as the first layer, or they are too difficult to spread.

*   You can add just about anything to this dish—olives, bell peppers, green chiles, and avocados. You can omit lettuce or other vegetables you don't have. You can use cheddar cheese, jack cheese or both.

Side by Side

Serve with warm corn tortillas and butter, pinto beans or refried beans, and a lightly dressed green salad. Fresh fruit makes a nice additional side.

Tex-Mex Dinner in a Pan

Ingredients

1 onion, chopped

1 lb ground beef

2 small zucchinis or 1 medium zucchini, sliced thin

1 cup frozen corn kernels

1 14.5-oz can sliced stewed tomatoes

1 pkg taco or enchilada seasoning

1 c water

1 c instant rice

Directions

Cook rice in water in a covered bowl in the microwave. Brown onion with ground beef and seasoning. When meat is almost done, add zucchini, tomatoes and corn and continue cooking until meat is done. Add rice and stir well.

Preparation Time: 15 minutes

*   If you do not have taco seasoning, you can substitute a blend of 1 teaspoon chili powder (or, if you prefer it less spicy, 1/2 teaspoon chili powder and 1/2 teaspoon paprika), 1 teaspoon garlic powder, 1/2 teaspoon cumin, and 1/2 teaspoon salt. You can also add some onion powder and oregano.

*   If you want to cook the entire dish in the pan without precooking the rice, you can do this but add 5 to 10 minutes simmer time with the pan covered so the rice can absorb the water and juice.

*   Garnish with sliced avocado, cilantro, cherry tomatoes, or sliced bell pepper. Or, sprinkle with 1/2 cup grated cheddar or cheddar/jack cheese and cover until melted. Then serve.

Side by Side

Fresh fruit and a small green salad complement this dish well. Light or creamy dressing as you choose works fine. Serve with refried beans spiked with a little grated cheddar and sour cream.

Taco Salad

Ingredients

1 heart of romaine, chopped

1 c kidney beans, drained and rinsed

1 tomato, chopped

1 green onion, diced

1 c cheddar cheese, grated

1 c corn chips, crushed

Ranch dressing

Directions

Toss lettuce, beans, tomato and onion. Add cheese and chips and toss with ranch dressing.

Preparation Time: 10 minutes

*   Heart of romaine is suggested because you want your salad greens crunchy and romaine hearts give you a good blend of leafy green and crunchy. This salad can also be made well with iceberg lettuce. The preferred corn chip in our house is a Frito® but any tortilla chip can be used. If you want a little heartier salad, add a half pound of ground turkey or beef browned with a splash of garlic powder, salt and cumin. You can also add sliced black olives.

*   For a more low-fat version of this salad, toss salad ingredients with your favorite salsa as the dressing. Or use French dressing or a dressing made of two parts ranch dressing and one part salsa.

Side by Side

Serve this salad as a main dish with Spanish rice and refried beans on the side. It goes with Mexican pull-apart bread (page 42—see recipe notes) or green chili quesadillas (page 44). You can also simply serve it with garlic bread and sliced fruit.

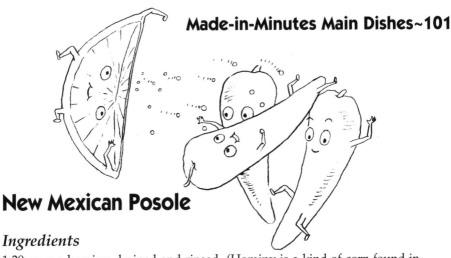

New Mexican Posole

Ingredients

1 29-oz can hominy, drained and rinsed (Hominy is a kind of corn found in
either the canned vegetable or Mexican food section of the market.)

4 green onions, diced

1/2 lb ground pork

1/2 t salt

1 t garlic powder

1/2 t ground cumin

2 T diced mild green chiles

1/2 lime

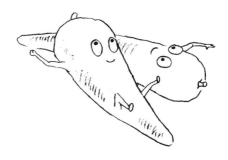

Directions

Brown pork with onions and seasonings over medium high heat. Rinse
hominy. Lower heat and add hominy and green chiles. Stir until hominy is
heated through. Squeeze with lime and serve. Serves 6.

Preparation Time: less than 10 minutes

*   This dish is quick and tasty. It is also a classic New Mexican Christmas
dish if you want to try it for a special holiday dinner with corn tortillas.

Side by Side

Serve this soup with warm corn tortillas and butter and mixed greens with
avocado dressing (page 107) or romaine with oranges and avocados (page
111). The black bean salad (page 114) is a good additional side. Another salad
side that is good is cut fresh fruit sprinkled with peanuts and dressed with
sweet and tangy dressing (page 106).

Swiss Enchiladas

Ingredients

1 T vegetable oil

4 boneless chicken breasts or thighs

1 onion, chopped

1 t garlic powder

1 7-oz can diced green chiles

Mild salsa verde

Sour cream

Grated jack or Swiss cheese, or half jack/half Swiss

Flour tortillas

1/2-3/4 c milk

Directions

Preheat oven to 400°. Sauté chicken, onion, garlic powder and chiles in skillet. Cut chicken into pieces as it cooks to speed up cooking process and get chicken into bite-size chunks. As pan dries out, add about 1/2 cup salsa verde. When chicken is fully cooked, set out six to eight tortillas, skillet of meat and remaining ingredients for enchilada assembly. Spray 9 by 13 inch baking pan with non-stick spray. Put a large tablespoon full of meat mixture into center of tortilla, top with handful of cheese, tablespoon of salsa verde, and dollop of sour cream. Roll and fold tortilla around filling and place fold side down in baking pan. Repeat until pan is full—six to eight enchiladas. Sprinkle more cheese over top and drizzle with salsa verde and milk. Bake in oven for about 20 minutes or until cheese is melted. If cheese begins to brown before baking is done, cover with aluminum foil.

Preparation Time: 15 minutes working time/20 minutes baking time

Side by Side

Serve with Caribbean black beans (page 124) and a romaine and spinach salad dressed with avocado dressing (page 107) or sweet and tangy dressing (page 106). Sliced fresh fruit is also good with this dish.

Layered Cheese Enchiladas

Ingredients

15-16 corn tortillas

1 24-oz jar mild picante sauce or red salsa

6 c shredded cheddar or longhorn cheese

5 green onions, chopped

1/2 diced red bell pepper (optional)

Directions

Preheat oven to 400°. Layer ingredients in a 9 by 13 inch baking dish, beginning with about a quarter of the salsa. Then layer tortillas, cheese, green onions (and bell pepper) and drizzle with picante sauce. Make two complete layers and then top with tortillas, salsa and cheese. Bake for 20 to 30 minutes—until cheese is melted through. Garnish with sour cream, chopped tomatoes, onions, and red bell pepper.

Preparation Time: less than 10 minutes working time/20-30 minutes baking time

Side by Side

Serve with sliced fresh fruit or greens and diced vegetables such as broccoli, zucchini, and celery dressed with sweet and tangy dressing (page 106).

Scrumptious Salads & Sides

Could that be your family asking for seconds of salad and vegetables? Unbelievable but true.

Sweet and Tangy Dressing

Ingredients

1 part red wine vinegar

1 part sugar

2 parts vegetable oil

Directions

Put ingredients in small airtight container and shake vigorously. Dress salad immediately. Dressing will last for a few days in the refrigerator, but shake it before using.

Preparation Time: 5 minutes

*   Some good greens combinations for this dressing are as follows: romaine, green onions, tomatoes and twice as much avocado as seems appropriate; romaine, fresh basil leaves, mushrooms, red bell pepper and cucumbers; and romaine, fresh cilantro leaves, tomatoes and green onion.

*   This dressing can also be used over a fresh fruit salad for a change of pace.

*   A great cabbage salad (sometimes called sumi salad) can be made with this dressing and is a great addition to any meal or buffet table. The best part is that it takes only a couple minutes. Take a bag of shredded red or green cabbage. Mix it with 1/4 cup sliced or slivered almonds, diced green onion, 1/2 package broken up, uncooked ramen noodles and a sprinkle of toasted sesames seeds (optional). Toss with this dressing and serve immediately or within a half hour. After about 30 minutes the hard ramen noodles get soft and, while still good, are not at their best.

*   Another quick salad with similar flavors uses 1/8 cup red wine or rice vinegar mixed with 1/8 cup water and 1 tablespoon sugar as the dressing for thinly-sliced, peeled cucumbers. You can add diced chives or green onions for color. You can also serve cucumbers in plain rice wine which is available in the Asian foods section of many markets.

Avocado Dressing

Ingredients
1/2 medium avocado, mashed

1/4 c Italian dressing

Directions
Mash avocado and blend in Italian dressing. Dresses a salad for 4 to 6 people.

Preparation Time: less than 5 minutes

* This dressing is good with romaine, tomatoes, green onion, corn and sliced avocado.

* For dressing enough to serve a large party, mash about 4 avocados and blend into a bottle of Italian dressing.

Balsamic Vinaigrette

Ingredients
1/2 c olive oil

1/4 c balsamic vinegar

1 t sugar

Salt and pepper

Directions
Mix first three ingredients and sprinkle with salt and pepper. Whisk or shake in a spill proof container to blend before serving. Store unused dressing in the refrigerator. It will last several days.

Preparation Time: 5 minutes

* Good ingredients to use with this dressing are romaine, Gorgonzola, diced apples and walnuts, preferably sugar-glazed walnuts. This makes a great salad for company.

999 Island Dressing

Ingredients
1/2 c mayonnaise

2 T catsup

2 T pickle relish

Directions
Mix these ingredients to make your own Thousand Island dressing when you want a creamy dressing on greens or a spread for burgers.

Preparation Time: less than 5 minutes

*   Thousand Island dressing is handy to have around the house. Not only is it a child-friendly dressing for greens, it is also a great all-purpose spread for hamburgers and sandwiches.

*   Kids get a big kick out of making their own Thousand Island dressing and seem to think it's rather amazing that you can make something at home that they often see in a bottle.

*   Another version of Thousand Island dressing can be made by mixing 1/2 cup mayonnaise with 3 tablespoons bottled chili sauce. Chili sauce is found in the salad dressing section of the market, often next to the catsup and relish.

Parmesan Dressing

Ingredients

1/4 c mayonnaise

2 T finely grated Parmesan cheese

1/2 t Italian seasoning blend, parsley flakes, or oregano flakes

1 T milk

Directions

Mix dressing ingredients in a bowl and then toss into green salad or salad of mixed chopped vegetables such as corn, tomatoes, green onions, peas, mushrooms, and bell pepper.

Preparation Time: less than 5 minutes

*   This recipe provides the mixed dressing version of the dressing used on seven-layer salad. For anyone not familiar with a seven-layer salad, it is made by layering chopped lettuce, peas, cucumbers, green or red onions, and tomatoes in a large bowl. The top of the bowl is then sealed with mayonnaise onto which finely grated Parmesan cheese is sprinkled. The salad is good for make-ahead occasions as it will last overnight. It is served by cutting into the layers almost as you would cut a cake. It is quite tasty and usually very well received.

Mustard Vinaigrette

Ingredients

1/4 c vegetable oil

2 T red wine vinegar

1 T Dijon mustard

1 t sugar

Directions

Mix dressing ingredients in a cup and whisk with a fork or shake in an airtight container.

Preparation Time: 5 minutes

*   Use this dressing on mixed greens or fresh baby spinach, sliced mushrooms, and diced green onion.

*   You can make a quick honey mustard dressing by combining 1/4 cup honey, 1 tablespoon Dijon mustard, 1/4 teaspoon paprika, 1/2 teaspoon garlic powder, 2 tablespoons apple cider vinegar and 1 tablespoon apple juice. Whisk or shake ingredients and toss with your favorite greens.

Romaine with Oranges and Avocados

Ingredients
1 orange, peeled and chopped

1 avocado, peeled and chopped

Romaine lettuce torn into pieces

Dressing
1/3 c plain yogurt

3 T orange juice

1 t honey

Directions
Cut fresh fruit and greens into bowl. Mix creamy orange dressing, drizzle over salad and toss.

Preparation Time: 5 minutes

*   For another version of creamy orange dressing which is a little tangier, mix 1/2 cup plain yogurt with 1-2 tablespoons of orange marmalade.

Roasted Red Pepper and Gorgonzola Salad

Ingredients
Mixed salad greens

Roasted red bell pepper

Gorgonzola

Balsamic vinaigrette (page 107)

Directions
Place mixed greens in a bowl. Drain roasted bell pepper from jar and cut into slender strips. Crumble Gorgonzola into salad. Toss with balsamic vinaigrette.

Preparation Time: less than 10 minutes

*	You can purchase roasted bell pepper in a jar or roast your own. To roast your own, hold pepper on a long fork over gas range fire to soften pepper. Or, roast peppers in the broiler. Peel off roasted skin.

*	Candied walnuts or pecans make this salad special. You can carmelize your own quickly. Cover 1 pound nuts with boiling water. Let sit for two or three minutes while you put 1/2 cup granulated sugar in a plastic bag. Drain nuts and, while still hot, pour them into bag. Close bag and toss nuts quickly to coat with sugar. Put nuts into strainer to get rid of excess liquid. Spread nuts on cookie sheet and bake at 400° for 15 minutes. At about 7 minutes, move nuts around on cookie sheet to avoid scorching.

Avocado and Onions

Ingredients

1 large avocado, peeled and sliced

1 red onion, sliced thin

1 tomato, chopped

Sweet and tangy dressing (page 106)

Directions

Place 3 to 4 slices of avocado on each plate. Top with thin slices of onion (or if you prefer, diced onion) and chopped tomatoes. Drizzle with sweet and tangy dressing. Serves 4.

Preparation Time: 5 minutes

*   While the thinly sliced onions look lovely, this salad is much easier to eat and enjoy if both the onion and the tomatoes are chopped. The salad is quick to make and a colorful visual feast. It goes well with Caribbean or Mexican cuisine.

*   To make this salad even more quickly, you can dress the vegetable ingredients with a bottled red wine vinaigrette dressing.

Black Bean Salad

Ingredients

1 15-oz can black beans, drained and rinsed

1 9-oz can kernel corn, drained

2 green onions, chopped

1 tomato, chopped

2 T fresh cilantro, chopped

1 T olive oil

1 T red wine vinegar

Juice of 1/2 lime

1/4 t garlic powder

Salt and pepper to taste

Directions

Mix first five ingredients in bowl. Drizzle and sprinkle remaining ingredients into bowl and stir gently. Chill if you do not eat immediately. Serve alone or on a bed of lettuce.

Preparation Time: 5 minutes

*   Everything goes into one bowl with this recipe. There is no need to make the dressing separately.

*   This salad can make a nice meal for lunch. Serve it on a bed of lettuce with sliced avocados.

*   If you prefer, you can dress the first five ingredients with sweet and tangy salad dressing (page 106).

*   Here's another tasty, quick black bean salad: Toss kernel corn, diced green onion, drained black beans, chopped red bell pepper, and tomato—about 4 to 5 cups of total veggies. Dress with 2 tablespoons red wine vinegar and 2 tablespoons fresh diced cilantro. Adjust the vinegar used to the amount of vegetables in your salad. If you use more vegetables, add more vinegar and cilantro. It's the fresh cilantro that makes the difference. Without it, the salad is flat. With it, it's tasty as can be and healthy, too.

Two-Bean Salad

Ingredients

1 15-oz can black beans, drained

1 15-oz can white kidney beans, drained

1 small bell pepper, diced

1/2 sweet onion, diced or 3 diced green onions

1/4 t salt

1/2 t black pepper

2 T sweet pickle relish

1 T balsamic vinegar

Directions

Rinse and drain beans. Add diced vegetables, salt and pepper. Mix well. Add pickle relish and vinegar and stir again to blend. Serve immediately or, if you refrigerate and serve later, you may want to splash on a bit more balsamic vinegar and/or pickle relish to taste. This salad serves 4--6.

Preparation Time: 5 minutes

*   This is a fun salad because you can modify it to go with thematic dinners. For example, if you use white and pink beans with red bell pepper, it is a Valentine salad. If you use black and white beans and orange and yellow bell pepper, it is an autumn masterpiece.

Pasta Salad with Feta Cheese

Ingredients

8 oz corkscrew pasta (fusilli)

2 tomatoes, chopped

2 green onions, chopped

1/2 bell pepper, chopped

1/3 c any other chopped vegetable of your choice such as cucumber or celery

2 oz herbed feta cheese, crumbled

1/2 t Italian seasoning

1 T olive oil

2 T red wine vinegar

Directions

While the pasta is cooking, cut your vegetables. To cool pasta quickly, run cold water over it. Put pasta, feta cheese and olive oil into bowl with vegetables. Toss lightly. Add Italian seasoning and red wine vinegar. Toss until well mixed.

Preparation Time: 5 minutes working time/15 minutes pasta cooking time

*   Cut down on the time it takes to make this salad by using a smaller pasta than corkscrew or fusilli. Feel free to substitute vegetables if you don't have one of those listed above. Other good additions to this salad are broccoli flowerets (chopped small), peas, and zucchini. Splash on more vinegar if you need to enhance the tang of the dressing.

*   To turn this into a main dish, add tuna. If you have tuna in oil, use the tuna oil and all and delete the olive oil. Then splash on vinegar.

*   Another great quick salad that takes advantage of crumbled feta cheese is made like this: Cut up green onions, tomato, and cucumbers. Add a few of your favorite small pitted olives. Crumble in your feta and dress with two parts olive oil, one part red wine vinegar and 1/2 teaspoon oregano flakes. It's very good and healthy.

Green Pea Salad

Ingredients

1 lb frozen peas, thawed

1 green onion, diced

1/4 c sugar

1/4 c red wine vinegar

1/4 t garlic powder

Dash red pepper flakes

Directions

To thaw frozen peas quickly, rinse under hot water. Let sit for a couple minutes while you mix sugar, vinegar, garlic powder and red pepper flakes in bowl. Rinse peas again with cold water. Place in bowl and toss with green onion and dressing.

Preparation Time: 5 minutes

Warm Rice Salad with Shrimp

Ingredients

2 c cooked rice

1/2 lb cooked salad or small shrimp, thawed

1 stalk celery, diced

Dressing

1/4 c vegetable oil

1/4 c lime juice

1/8 c brown sugar, packed

1/4 t red pepper flakes

Directions

Mix rice, shrimp and celery. Mix oil, juice, sugar and pepper flakes. Dress salad with about 1/2 of the dressing. If you do not serve immediately, use remaining dressing to freshen salad before serving. Serve warm or cold.

Preparation Time: 10 minutes

*   To add more crunch, this recipe is good with 1/2 cup carmelized walnuts which are now available in the specialty or baking section of many markets. Or, make your own with the recipe on page 112.

*   This recipe takes ten minutes if you cook your own minute-style rice as part of the process. If you are using leftover rice, the whole salad takes only about 5 minutes to put together.

Broccoli Salad

Ingredients

2 c diced broccoli flowerets

1 green onion, diced

1/4 c + 2 T dry roasted sunflower seeds

1/2 c dried cranberries

1/4 c mayonnaise

1 T sugar

1 t red wine vinegar

Directions

Dice broccoli and onion and put in bowl with sunflower seeds and cranberries. Add remaining ingredients directly into bowl and stir briskly to mix salad dressing ingredients into salad.

Preparation Time: 5 minutes

*   This surprising combination of ingredients makes a winning salad that is a big hit with nearly everyone.

*   You can serve this salad immediately or refrigerate it so that it is chilled when served. It is even better chilled.

*   You can substitute dried cherries or raisins for the cranberries. Some people like it with half diced broccoli and half diced cauliflower.

*   The dressing for this salad (i.e., mayonnaise, sugar and red wine vinegar) is also great for coleslaw. You might add a dash of celery seed to the dressing for coleslaw.

Corn Salad

Ingredients

1 10-oz bag frozen kernel corn, thawed

1/2 red onion, diced (or 2 green onions, diced)

1/2 red bell pepper, diced (optional)

2-3 T red wine vinegar

1 t sugar

1/2 t ground cumin

1/2 t garlic powder

1/4 t salt

Directions

Thaw corn by running cold water over it. While corn thaws, dice onion and bell pepper if you use it. Add onion and pepper to corn. Add remaining ingredients directly to vegetables, sprinkling them randomly. Toss and serve. Serves about 6 and refrigerates well.

Preparation Time: 5 minutes working time/refrigerate as desired

*   This is a good make ahead salad. You can make it early in the day or the day ahead.

*   An alternate corn salad that is also very quick is a corn and pea salad. The ingredients are 2 cans white corn (drained), 1 cup frozen petite peas (thawed), 2 cups diced green onion, and 1/2 cup mayonnaise. Mix all ingredients and add salt and pepper to taste. An alternative dressing for this salad is 2 parts ranch dressing with 1 part sour cream. Or, use this modified ranch dressing to toss peas and onions with crumbled bacon bits.

Orange-Glazed Carrots

Ingredients
1 lb baby carrots

1/3 c orange marmalade

2 T butter, melted

1 t Dijon mustard

Pinch ground ginger

Directions
Microwave or steam carrots. While the carrots are cooking, melt butter in microwave or stovetop and stir in remaining ingredients. When carrots are done, drain them and stir in the marmalade glaze. Serve immediately. They can sit and be reheated without doing them much harm.

Preparation Time: 10-12 minutes (less if you use frozen carrots)

*   Using frozen carrot rounds cuts the preparation time on this recipe by about half because they cook faster than fresh baby carrots.

*   It's even faster to simply steam and drain the carrots; then stir in the marmalade and a pinch of ginger until melted. And they're ready to serve.

Broccoli and Mushroom Casserole

Ingredients

1 lb frozen broccoli flowerets, thawed

1 green onion, chopped

1 c mushrooms, sliced

1 can cream of mushroom soup

1/2 c mayonnaise (optional)

2 c croutons

1 c grated cheddar cheese

Directions

Preheat oven to 450°. Mix all ingredients in bowl. Put into 9 by 13 inch baking dish. Bake for 15 minutes. Serves 6.

Preparation Time: 5 minutes working time/15 minutes baking time

*   You can substitute a small can of mushrooms (drained) for fresh mushrooms. You can use a tablespoon of frozen chopped or fresh chopped onion for the green onion.

*   You can substitute sweet mayonnaise-style salad dressing for the mayonnaise if you prefer a sweeter taste.

*   You can omit croutons or add a breast or thigh of chopped cooked chicken to this vegetable casserole. The croutons you use can be unseasoned or seasoned.

Couscous and Carrots

Ingredients

1 c couscous

1 c water

1 carrot, grated

1 small onion, chopped

2 T sliced almonds

2 T butter or margarine

Directions

Heat water to boiling. Meanwhile, sauté carrot, onion, and almonds in butter until onions are translucent. Add couscous to boiling water, turn off heat, and cover with lid for five minutes. Fluff couscous with fork, stir in sautéed vegetables and serve.

Preparation Time: 5-10 minutes

Caribbean Black Beans

Ingredients

1 T vegetable oil

1 small onion, chopped

1 clove garlic, minced or 1 t garlic powder

2 15-oz cans black beans

3/4 c orange juice

1 T salsa or hot sauce (optional)

Directions

Sauté onion and garlic in oil over medium high heat. Drain and rinse beans. Add to pan with orange juice and hot sauce. Heat while mashing slightly in pan to absorb liquid.

Preparation Time: 5 minutes

Almond Asparagus

Ingredients

1 bunch asparagus (about 20 spears)

1 T and 1 t vegetable oil

1/4 c sliced almonds

1/4 c water

1 t sugar

1/4 t salt

Fresh cracked pepper

1/2 lemon

Directions

Cut asparagus into thirds. Sauté almonds in 1 teaspoon oil over high heat until toasted (about 1 minute). Remove almonds. Put remaining oil in skillet with asparagus, water, sugar, salt and pepper. Stir quickly over high heat for no more than a minute. Lower heat and cover for about 3 minutes or until asparagus is tender. Squeeze lemon over asparagus. Transfer to serving plate and sprinkle with almonds.

Preparation Time: less than 10 minutes

*   Another classy, quick way to serve asparagus is with garlic butter drizzled over the top. Steam asparagus (or other vegetable of your choice—broccoli works well, too). Combine 1/2 teaspoon crushed garlic or 1 minced garlic clove with two tablespoons butter for 1/2 to 3/4 pound of vegetables. Drizzle garlic butter over hot veggies and sprinkle to taste with salt and fresh cracked pepper.

*   Another nut-crunchy vegetable dish can be made using frozen green beans and cashews to add the crunch. Steam one pound green beans. While they are steaming, melt 2 to 3 tablespoons butter with 1/4 teaspoon salt and 1/4 teaspoon fresh cracked paper. When green beans are cooked, toss with butter mixture and 1/2 cup crushed cashews. This one takes only about five minutes but is special because of the nuts. You can substitute almonds for the cashews if that's what you have on hand.

Desserts in a Dash

Okay, dessert IS a treat—but it doesn't have to take all day to make. These desserts are so easy your kids will be making them. Pretty soon they'll be making dinner, too.

Peaches Caramel

Ingredients
2 T butter

1/3 c packed light brown sugar

1 large can sliced peaches in heavy syrup, drained

2 T heavy or whipping cream

Dash cinnamon

Directions
Drain peaches and reserve liquid. Melt butter in large skillet over medium heat. Add brown sugar and 1/4 cup reserved syrup. Stir constantly to melt sugar. Lower heat slightly and add peaches, cinnamon and cream. Stir until thick and golden. Serve over ice cream or in bowl with dollop of sour cream or whipped cream. Serves 4 to 6.

Preparation Time: 5-10 minutes

* You can add a tablespoon of rum or brandy to the sauce when you add the fruit.

* You can make this dessert with fresh fruit. Use five or six large peaches, sliced and peeled. Slicing and peeling the fresh fruit obviously adds to the preparation time.

* You can use margarine instead of butter and half-and-half instead of whipping cream. You can delete the whipping cream entirely for a slightly different sauce. In this case, you may use more peach syrup.

* You can substitute 3 sliced bananas for peaches and delete whipping cream for a bananas foster-style dessert. To make bananas foster, melt a half cube butter with 1/4 cup packed brown sugar. Add sliced bananas and a dash of nutmeg and stir over medium heat until sauce is clear—three to five minutes. Serve the caramel bananas with vanilla ice cream. You can flavor the bananas foster with a dash of rum or brandy if you like.

Fresh Berries and Sweetened Sour Cream

Ingredients

1/2 c sour cream

2-3 T brown sugar

1/4 t ground nutmeg

Fresh strawberries, raspberries and blueberries

Directions

Mix first three ingredients. Place in a bowl and surround with fresh fruit for dipping.

Preparation Time: less than 5 minutes

*   Sliced fresh fruits such as kiwi, peaches and nectarines also make nice dipping fruits for this dessert. Using sliced fruits rather than berries increases the preparation time due to the slicing and peeling involved.

*   Another way to serve this dessert is to skip the nutmeg and skip the mixing. Simply place a bowl of sour cream and a bowl of brown sugar out with your fruit for diners to dip into as they choose.

*   An alternate way to use the dipping sauce is to dress fresh red seedless grapes with it. It is a cool and refreshing dessert that is light but satisfying. Serve with a sprig of fresh mint.

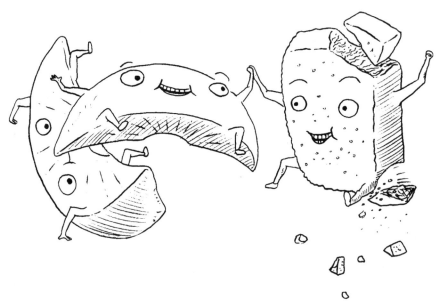

Fruity Vanilla Parfait

Ingredients

Fresh blueberries

Fresh chopped peaches

Crumbled biscotti or shortbread cookies

2 8-oz containers vanilla yogurt

Ingredients

Make this dessert by layering ingredients in 4 tall glasses. Begin in each with a spoonful of vanilla yogurt. Add some pieces of each kind of fruit. Top with crumbled cookies. Repeat layers again. Serve immediately so cookies retain crunchiness.

Preparation Time: less than 5 minutes

*   When you do not have fresh fruit in season, you can modify this recipe by using drained mandarin oranges and drained pineapple chunks.

*   This dessert can also be made with fresh strawberries and raspberries.

*   You can substitute a favorite granola for the biscotti or shortbread.

Strawberry Almond Swirl

Ingredients

1 10-oz package frozen strawberries with sugar, thawed

2 cups plain yogurt

1 t vanilla

2 t almond extract

Slivered almonds

Directions

If strawberries are not thawed, thaw them in the microwave. Put yogurt, vanilla and almond extract into a bowl and mix. Fold in strawberries gently so that the yogurt and strawberries make a swirl effect. Serve in glass bowls with almonds on top.

Preparation Time: 5 minutes

*   If you prefer to use fresh berries, chop them. If you use fresh, unsweetened berries, add a few tablespoons sugar to the yogurt along with the flavorings for every cup of yogurt you use. How much sugar you use is a matter of personal taste.

*   You can also use thawed frozen raspberries for this recipe. Again, depending upon the sugar in your fruit, you can adjust how much sugar, if any, to add to your yogurt.

*   For a change of pace, top with granola rather than almonds.

Yogurt Pie

Ingredients
1 8-oz blended peach or raspberry yogurt

1 small container frozen whipped topping, thawed

1 prepared graham cracker or shortbread crust

Directions
Fold yogurt into whipped topping and pour into crust. Freeze for at least 30 minutes before serving.

Preparation Time: less than 5 minutes working time; 30+ minutes freezing time

*   To enhance the presentation of this easy pie, you can decorate it right before serving with fresh fruit slices or by drizzling thinned jam over it.

*   You can make this pie with other yogurts of your choice such as strawberry or blueberry. If you use blueberry, you might want to put a half can of blueberry pie filling in the bottom of the pie before spooning on the cream filling. Alternately, put sliced bananas on the crust before adding the filling.

Pineapple Dump Cake

Ingredients
1 box yellow cake mix

1 or 2 sticks butter (1/4 or 1/2 lb), depending how rich you want the cake

16 oz crushed pineapple with juice

1/2 c chopped pecans (optional)

Directions
Preheat oven to 350°. Spray nonstick cooking spray on inside of a 7 x 11-inch baking dish. Spread dry cake mix evenly on bottom of baking dish. Cut butter into pats and dot it over the cake mix. Sprinkle with nuts if you choose to use them. Drizzle pineapple as evenly as possible over the preceding layers. Bake for about 30 minutes or until lightly golden at edges. Stir ingredients slightly about halfway through to mix dry cake mix with moist ingredients. Serves 8.

Preparation Time: 5 minutes working time; 30 minutes baking time

* If you don't have a cake mix, this recipe will serve as a substitute: 1 1/2 cups flour, 1 cup sugar, 1/2 teaspoon salt, and 2 teaspoons baking powder.

* This dessert is great by itself, but a real treat with vanilla ice cream.

* To make this dessert for a family of four, cut the ingredients by half and bake in an 8-inch cake dish. Baking time is then shortened to about 20 minutes.

* This easy dessert works well with a variety of fruits. Try half pineapple with half cherry pie filling and almonds or pecans. Chopped peaches seasoned with cinnamon are another delicious choice.

* A holiday version of this dessert substitutes pumpkin for the fruit. If you choose to do this, prepare the pumpkin filling as you would for a pie and pour it over the cake mix and butter. Again, stir the dessert halfway through the cooking process which is finished when a knife inserted into the pumpkin comes out clean.

Peanut Butter Cookies

Ingredients

1 c creamy peanut butter

1 c sugar

1 large egg

1 t baking powder

Dash cinnamon

Directions

Preheat oven to 350°. Mix all ingredients together. Form into one inch balls. Place on ungreased cookie sheet and press crossways with a fork. Sprinkle with extra granulated sugar, if you choose. Bake for about 10 minutes. Makes about 30 cookies.

Preparation Time: 5-10 minutes working time; 10 minutes baking time

*   Really, this is not a mistake. These cookies have no flour.

*   If you want to make bite-size cookies, make each cookie half as big and shorten the baking time to between 5 and 7 minutes.

*   This cookie is also yummy with 3/4 cup chocolate chips added. Mini-chip morsels work best. If you make peanut butter chippers, don't press the cookies before baking and add 2 to 3 minutes to the baking time. Adding the chips lets you make about 3 to 3 1/2 dozen cookies.

Papaya and Sorbet

Ingredients

1 papaya, seeded, peeled and sliced

Mango sorbet

Passion fruit sorbet

1/2 c mild pepper jelly

Juice of 1 lime

Directions

Prepare papaya. Place two to three slices on each plate. Top with small scoop of each sorbet. Mix lime juice into pepper jelly with a fork. Drizzle over sorbet. Makes 4 to 6 servings depending upon how much papaya each person is served.

Preparation Time: 5 minutes

*   You can save the peeling time if you simply cut the papaya into wedges after seeding it. Place the sorbet scoops on a wedge or half papaya.

*   If you only have hot pepper jelly, you might try using a blend of half pepper jelly and half peach or apricot jam mixed with your lime juice. This will cool the hot sparks for those who are sensitive to spicy foods.

*   Another excellent, easy, and light dessert is to simply slice a chilled papaya in half and seed it. Squeeze fresh lime juice over the fruit and serve. Garnish with a mint leaf if desired. It is delicious and the way papaya is often served in Hawaii.

Ambrosia

Ingredients

1 10-oz can mandarin oranges, drained

1 8-oz can pineapple (tidbits or crushed), drained

1 banana, sliced

4 oz cream cheese, softened

2 T sugar

2 T milk

1/4 c shredded coconut

Directions

Mix cream cheese with sugar. Then add milk, one tablespoon at a time, and stir until smooth. Add fruit and coconut, stir, and chill.

Preparation Time: 5 minutes

* You can add toasted pecans or almonds to this recipe or delete the coconut if you choose. You can also substitute fresh orange pieces for the mandarin oranges.

Coconut Orange Cream

Ingredients
8 soft coconut macaroons

1/4 c orange juice

1 c whipping cream

1 T powdered sugar

1/2 t vanilla

Directions
Break macaroons into pieces and soak in orange juice. Stir occasionally while you prepare remaining ingredients. Whip heavy cream with sugar and vanilla. Fold whipping cream into macaroon mixture and serve.

Preparation Time: 5 minutes

* For another super quick whipped cream dessert, mix a jar of strained baby food apricots or prunes with whipped cream, chill, and serve. You can also add a little powdered sugar. The kids love this one.

Kinda Kheer

Ingredients

3/4 c couscous

3/4 c water

1 c evaporated milk

1/8 c brown sugar, packed (2 T)

1/4 c slivered almonds, toasted

1 t almond flavoring

Directions

Make couscous according to package directions. Or, mix equal parts boiling water and couscous, cover, and let stand for 3 to 5 minutes. While couscous is cooking, toast almonds in a dry pan for 1 to 2 minutes. Mix milk, sugar, almond flavoring and almonds. Fluff couscous with fork and pour milk mixture over it.

Preparation Time: 5 minutes

*   This dessert is a variation on Indian rice pudding called kheer. You can add raisins to it if you like things fruity. You can also make it with leftover rice.

*   Leftovers reheated in the microwave serve well for breakfast.

*   This is a good dessert for kids when you don't want to do dessert because it satisfies that sweet tooth but is healthy and has only a little sugar.

Orange Ice Cream

Ingredients

1 c heavy cream

1 c milk

1 t vanilla

1 c sugar

2 T lemon juice

1 c orange juice

Directions

Put all ingredients in bowl and stir to help sugar dissolve. Freeze in bowl. Stir occasionally during the freezing process. Ready to serve in 2 to 4 hours. Serves 4 to 6.

Preparation Time: 5 minutes working time; 2-4 hours freezing time

*   This ice cream is good topped with fresh berries.

*   You can also use this recipe in electric or hand-crank ice cream freezers.

*   Try other juices of your choice with this recipe.

Lime Pie

Ingredients

1 qt vanilla ice cream, softened

1/2 can frozen limeade concentrate

2-3 drops green food coloring

Graham cracker crust

Directions

Mix the ice cream and limeade. Add food coloring until your pie filling is as green as you want it. Spoon mixture into pie crust and freeze for 45 minutes to 1 hour.

Preparation Time: less than 10 minutes working time; 1 hour chilling time

*   To make an orange pie variation, use 1 pint vanilla ice cream and 1 pint orange sherbet for the filling. Fold the ice cream and sherbet together in a bowl. Blend until swirled, but not completely mixed. Spoon filling into pie crust and freeze.

*   Here's a good recipe for a cookie/graham crust if you have the time or inclination to make your own. For an 8-inch pie plate, use two cups crumbs (graham cracker, chocolate cookie or sugar cookie), 1/4 cup butter and 1/4 cup granulated sugar. Mix ingredients well. Press into the pie plate and bake for 10 minutes at 425°. Cool and fill.

Ice Cream de Menthe

Ingredients

4 brownies, slices chocolate pound cake or large chewy chocolate cookies

4 scoops vanilla ice cream

4 T creme de menthe

4 T chocolate sauce

Directions

Place a brownie on each plate. Top with a scoop of vanilla ice cream and drizzle with creme de menthe and chocolate sauce.

Preparation Time: less than 5 minutes if you use readymade brownies, cake, or cookies

* If you bake your own brownies for this dessert, you need to add about 30 minutes to the preparation time, but this can be done well in advance. A quick brownie recipe is 1/2 cup melted butter, 1/2 cup dark chocolate syrup such as Hershey's®, 1 cup sugar, 1 teaspoon vanilla, 2 eggs, and 3/4 cup flour. Mix the ingredients into each other in the order listed. Bake in a 7 by 11 inch baking pan greased with non-stick cooking spray. Bake at 350° for about 30 minutes.

* A variation on this dessert is to spoon crushed pineapple or pineapple snack wedges over vanilla ice cream and then drizzle it with creme de menthe. Skip the brownie or serve it on a slice of pound cake.

* Another quick, but tasty, ice cream dessert to remember is peach melba. Make it like this: Warm raspberry jam with a little water to thin. You can do this in a saucepan over low heat, stirring constantly, or in a microwave on high for 15 seconds and stir. Place a peach half (peeled fresh or canned) on each plate. Top with one scoop vanilla ice cream. Drizzle raspberry jam over ice cream and top each with a teaspoon of slivered almonds. You can fancy up your raspberry jam a bit by using a teaspoon of Amaretto or Grand Marnier as your thinning liquid.

Raspberry Trifle

Ingredients
1/2 bundt angel food cake (about 6 ounces), torn into 1-inch pieces

1 5.1-oz package instant vanilla pudding mix

3 c milk

1 c raspberry preserves

2-3 c non-dairy whipped topping

Directions
Whisk pudding mix with milk and set aside. Tear cake into 1-inch pieces and use half of the pieces to line bottom of 8-inch square pan or bowl that has 3-inch sides. Spread half of pudding on cake. Beat preserves slightly with a fork and spread half of preserves on cake. Spread half of whipped topping over preserves. Repeat layers finishing with whipped topping that seals in layers. Refrigerate until ready to serve. Serves 8 to 10.

Preparation Time: less than 15 minutes

* You can make this dessert fancier and still keep it easy by using real whipped cream instead of whipped topping. Just whip up 1 cup whipping cream with 1 tablespoon powdered sugar.

* You can substitute prepared pudding such as tapioca or make your own cooked vanilla pudding and cool.

* For a grown-up flavor, add a couple teaspoons of sherry or orange-flavored liqueur to the preserves.

* Another adaptation is to use sponge or pound cake. If you use pound cake, you can cut it into 1/2-inch slices and line the pan with these. If you choose, paint the cake with thawed frozen lemonade mix and then layer your puddings, preserves and whipped toppings. If you use the lemonade idea, try blueberry or blackberry for your trifle preserves.

Strawberry Fluff

Ingredients

1 10-oz package sliced frozen strawberries, thawed

1 2.75-oz (small) package strawberry gelatin

1/2 c water

6 oz angel food cake, torn into 1-inch pieces

1 8-oz carton non-dairy whipped topping

Directions

Tear cake into small pieces. Thaw strawberries (if you use the microwave, try high for about 2 minutes). Heat water on high. When it boils, mix in gelatin until dissolved. Add thawed strawberries and stir. Fold half whipped topping into strawberry mixture. Fold other half into torn cake pieces. Fold strawberry mixture into cake mixture and blend gently. Pour into 8 by 8-inch pan and chill until set.

Preparation Time: 5-10 minutes working time; 1 hour chilling time

Chocolate Banana Cream Pie

Ingredients

1 3.8-oz (small) chocolate pudding mix

1 c milk

1 c whipped topping

4 oz cream cheese

1/4 c sugar

1/2 c sour cream

1 banana, sliced

1 prepared graham cracker crust

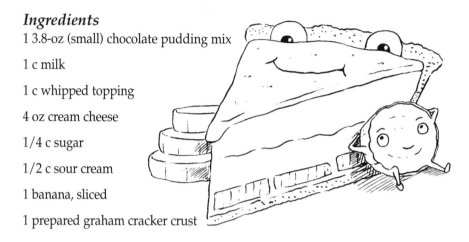

Directions

Whisk or shake pudding mix with milk and let set. Cream sugar and cream cheese. Add sour cream to cream cheese mixture, 1 heaping tablespoon at a time. Add whipped topping to pudding mixture and fold this mixture into the cream cheese mixture. Slice banana and layer on the bottom of the crust. Top with chocolate cream cheese mixture and refrigerate.

Preparation Time: 10 minutes working time; 20-30 minutes chilling time

* This pie can be eaten immediately after preparation, but cuts more nicely if chilled.

* This pie can be topped with whipped topping or whipped cream, if you desire.

* You can substitute vanilla pudding for chocolate pudding for a change of pace.

* Another modification of this recipe is to delete the banana and use cherry pie filling for the fruit. If you do this, spread the cream cheese mixture into the crust first and top with cherry pie filling.

Cream Cheese Pie

Ingredients

12 oz cream cheese, softened

1/4 c brown sugar, packed

1/4 c granulated sugar

1 t vanilla

2 eggs

3/4 c sour cream

1 prepared graham cracker crust

Extra granulated sugar

Directions

Preheat oven to 375°. Beat sugars into cream cheese with a fork. Add 1/2 teaspoon vanilla and beat again. Break eggs into a separate cup and beat slightly. Pour eggs a little at a time into the cream cheese mixture and beat until smooth. Pour into crust and bake for 20 to 30 minutes. While the pie is baking, mix 2 tablespoons granulated sugar and 1/2 teaspoon vanilla into sour cream. When pie is done (firm through the middle), spread sour cream mixture over top of pie and bake for additional 5 minutes. Remove from oven, cool, and refrigerate for at least an hour before serving.

Preparation Time: 15 minutes working time/25-35 minutes baking time; 1 hour chilling time

* This pie can be topped with cherry or blueberry pie filling instead of the sour cream mixture or in addition to the sour cream mixture.

* Many people prefer to bake cheesecake in a pan of water in the oven. This helps prevent the cake from drying out.

Banana Blueberry Cream Pie

Ingredients

1 prepared cookie crust

1 banana, sliced

4 oz cream cheese, softened

1/4 c sugar

1/2 c sour cream

4 oz whipped topping

1 can blueberry pie filling

Directions

Layer sliced banana on the crust. Mix cream cheese with sugar until soft and thoroughly mixed. Fold in sour cream. Gently blend in whipped topping. Spread this mixture over bananas. Cover with blueberry pie filling. Refrigerate until ready to serve.

Preparation Time: less than 15 minutes working time; 30 minutes chilling time

* This pie can be served immediately, but cutting it is easier after chilling.

* You can substitute cherry pie filling for the blueberry, if you prefer.

Index

147